EASY SEWING
Stretch Fabrics

EDITORIAL
Craft Editor: Tonia Todman
Fashion Designer: Sally Pereira
Text: Alison Magney
Editor: Sheridan Carter
Editorial Co-ordinator: Margaret Kelly
UK Consultant: Norma Lane
Sewing Assistants: Paula McPhail, Martina Oprey

DESIGN AND PRODUCTION
Margie Mulray
Chris Hatcher

ILLUSTRATIONS
Greg Gaul

PHOTOGRAPHY
Jon Waddy

STYLIST
Sally Hirst

DESIGN AND PRODUCTION MANAGER
Nadia Sbisa

PUBLISHER
Philippa Sandall

Family Circle is a registered trademark of IPC
Magazines Ltd.
Published by J. B. Fairfax Press Pty Ltd by
arrangement with IPC Magazines Ltd

Easy Sewing Stretch Fabrics
ISBN 1 8634 3 026 1
Formatted by J.B. Fairfax Press Pty Ltd
Output by Adtype, Sydney
Printed by Toppan Printing Co, Hong Kong

Cover: Frank Pithers (Design), Sally Hirst (Styling),
Jon Waddy (Photography)

Distributed in the UK by J.B. Fairfax Ltd
9 Trinity Centre, Park Farm Estate,
Wellingborough, Northants.
Ph: (0933) 402330 Fax: (0933) 402234

Distributed in Australia by
Newsagents Direct Distributors
150 Bourke Road, Alexandria NSW 2015
Supermarket distribution by
Storewide Magazine Distributors
150 Bourke Road, Alexandria NSW 2015
Distributed internationally by
T.B. Clarke (Overseas) Pty Ltd
80 McLachlan Avenue
Rushcutters Bay NSW

CONTENTS

METRIC / IMPERIAL CONVERSION CHART	
CENTIMETRES	INCHES
1	3/8
1.5	5/8
2	3/4
2.5	1
3	1 1/4
5	2
30	12
91	36

Size Wise

This book has been divided to have the garment instructions and photographs at the front and the grid patterns at the back. In the instructions the patterns are referred to by number. Several patterns are multi-purpose and as such their numbers appear frequently. Some styles have been designed to be very roomy, and others have a close fit. Our patterns use standard sizing but please check with your tape measure before drawing the patterns you choose.

Getting Started

Welcome to stretch fabrics – where the living is easy (and the sewing is too!). The clothes of today are incredibly comfortable and easy to look after. They're smart, but casual, and fit as clothes have never done before. Think (if you can bear to) of the corsets and suspender belts of thirty or forty years ago. Women were pushed and pummelled into shape via breath-restricting contraptions so they could fit into the wasp-waisted dresses and skin-tight skirts of yesteryear.

And let's not forget men, who had their 'uniform' of belts and braces, ties and stiff collars – and a man always had to have his tailored coat handy, just in case. Children were mini-models of their parents, and they had the added burden of trying to keep clean!

Goodbye to all that, and good riddance! Today, fluid fabrics and casual designs fit in with **us**, not vice-versa. This book shows you how you can turn stretch fabrics into skirts, dresses, babies' basics, tracksuits, pyjamas, bath wraps – even swimsuits.

The beauty of it all is that you can be a complete novice, a raw beginner, and still be able to put together the patterns provided in our book. Stop shaking your head. No matter what minor catastrophes have befallen you before, this time you'll succeed.

Spend a few minutes of your time reading about the fabrics, the equipment and our patterns. You'll be dressing yourself and your family in beautiful outfits, saving money and expressing your creativity, in no time at all.

WHAT IS STRETCH FABRIC?

Take a look at one of your knitted jumpers. What do you see? Tiny stitches, all looped together, forming a piece of fabric. All the various bits of fabric are sewn together to make your jumper.

Stretch fabrics are similarly composed of tiny stitches looped together. All stretch fabrics share two qualities that make them justifiably beloved. They shed wrinkles easily (who wants to iron these days?); and they do not fray or unravel, making them easy and fuss-free to sew.

Most stretch fabrics only stretch one way – sideways. Lycra is an example of a two-way stretch fabric, which stretches both lengthways and sideways and is thus highly elastic and figure-hugging. Two-way stretch fabrics are used to sew active sportswear like swimsuits and leotards.

PREPARING STRETCH FABRIC

Begin as you mean to continue! If you're tough on clothes, always tossing them from washing machine to dryer, make sure you wash and dry your fabric in exactly that way before you start cutting it out. Any stretch fabric that's been in a dryer will shrink quite considerably, so buy at least a third more fabric than the pattern says you will need if merciless tumble-drying is your way of doing things! Once shrunk and pressed your fabric is ready to cut and sew.

LAYING OUT THE PATTERNS AND CUTTING OUT

✂ In the same way as you would for a woven fabric, follow the pattern piece grainlines carefully.

✂ Stretch fabrics can distort if they're allowed to hang off the edge of your table or other cutting-out

Find out how easy it is to make this warm and cosy sweatshirt on page 35

surface. Avoid slippery table tops.
✄ Use weights instead of pins to hold pattern pieces in place on the fabric. Saucers do the job well.
✄ To cut out, lay your fabric double, unless the fabric is particularly bulky in which case lay out a single layer only.

STABILISED SEAMS

When a 'stabilised seam' is called for in this book, we're asking you to sew a seam that will prevent stretching, not encourage it or 'go with it'. A shoulder seam, for example, should not stretch.

Stitch over narrow, pre-shrunk tape as you sew this kind of seam.

SEAMS

When joining pieces, use a narrow zigzag stitch (see 1). You can use a straight stitch if you like, but remember to stretch the fabric slightly while sewing it to provide built-in elasticity (see 2).

Most modern sewing machines offer a variety of 'stretch' stitches. At last, here's your chance to use some of them. Experiment to find out which is the best stretch stitch for your purpose.

NEEDLES, PINS AND SCISSORS

The natural enemy of stretch fabrics is the damaged machine needle. It can ladder the looped stitches we discussed earlier, as if your fabric were a cheap stocking! Mind you, blunt needles are just as bad, or worse. Remember, new needles are not a luxury!

Test out your machine needle on a small piece of fabric. If it's dubious, a ball-point needle is a good option. Pins too can be ball-point, while longer, glass-headed pins are also fine.

Serrated scissors will help grip the fabric as you're cutting out, but they're not essential.

Your tension shouldn't need adjusting, though it is best to sew a sample fabric piece first.

Make it a practice to use good-quality, synthetic sewing thread.

OVERLOCKERS

These machines are easily the newest and most exciting event in the sewing world for some time. Sure, commercial manufacturers have been using them for ages, but they are now an easily obtainable machine on the domestic market.

Overlocker machines trim and stitch fabric edges in just one process. They are virtually 'tailor-made' for the sewing of stretch fabrics and, once you see how clever they are, you'll find them indispensable for sewing woven fabrics too.

When you're ready to expand your sewing equipment, do the rounds of all the sewing-machine shops and try one yourself.

RIBBING

To make stretchy bands at a garment's neck, cuff or whatever, use ribbed fabric. The amount of stretch in a piece of ribbed fabric varies so you need to let your own common sense help you to 'guesti-mate' the size the ribbing should be. As a rule, it is better to be firmer than too loose.

Measure twice, cut once – in other words, pin-fit the ribbing to your figure before you cut. Heads, hands and bodies need to be able to slip through the ribbing with ease.

If you can't decide how long to cut your ribbing, start with a piece the length of the garment opening and add 2 cm for the seam. Pin-fit more accurately from there.

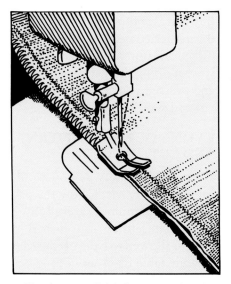

1 Simple seam finish for conventional sewing machines

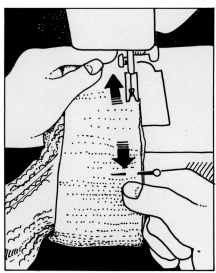

2 Stretching the fabric as you sew to provide built-in elasticity

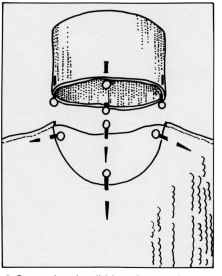

3 Quartering the ribbing piece and opening with pins

As a general principle, ribbing that is to go around necklines, wrists and hipbands can be cut to three-quarters of the size of the garment opening or width, but do check how much stretch there is in your particular piece of ribbing fabric. Cut the rib running vertically.

Purchased ribbing pieces like collars, cuffs and bands may be available in the appropriate colours. These are an alternative to ribbing by the metre.

CUTTING AND APPLYING RIBBING BANDS

Remember that the ribs in fabric run vertically. The width of the bands you cut will be up to you, or specified in the pattern.

Stitch the short ends of the ribbing together in a 1 cm seam. Fold the ribbing in half, wrong sides together. Divide the ribbing into four equal parts with pins, placing one pin at the seam line. Divide garment openings into four equal parts, placing pins accurately at the centre back and the centre front. Space other pins at halfway points in between (see 3).

Match the pins on the ribbing to the pins on the garment, noting that the ribbing is smaller than the garment opening (see 4). For a neckline, place the neckline ribbing seam precisely at centre back. Stitch the 1 cm seam with the ribbing on top of the garment, stretching the ribbing as necessary to fit the garment edge between pins (see 5).

Press the garment, but do **not** press the ribbing. If you do, it may stretch irretrievably out of shape.

HEMS

Handsew your hems if you like, but stretch fabrics allow for a much faster finishing method. Use your blind hem stitch, or simply turn up the hem and stitch, cutting away excess fabric close to the stitching when finished (see 6).

Use a twin needle trim, or top-stitch two rows as a feature. Always stretch the fabric as you sew to prevent the stitches from snapping when the fabric stretches. Another option is to use your narrowest zigzag for the hem finish.

NARROW BINDING

This can be used instead of a hem, facing or ribbing. It is not stretchy and should only be used where a contrast trim or feature is needed to finish something off.

If you want a good stretchy binding, cut your strip of material **across** the fabric because, as you will remember, stretch fabrics only stretch sideways.

Compare your measurements with those below. If your measurements are between two sizes, pick the larger size pattern. All our patterns include allowances for ease, style and a comfortable fit.

Babies and Children				
Size	Height	Chest	Waist	Hip
6 mths	68	47	48	48
2 years	92	53	51	56
4 years	104	57	53	60
6 years	122	63	56	66
12 years	158	77	63	86
Women	Average Height 168cm			
10		84	64	92
12		87	67	95
14		90	70	98
Men	Average Height 176cm			
M		96	84	102
L		100	86	106

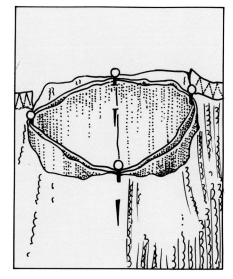

4 Pinning ribbing in place matching quarter points

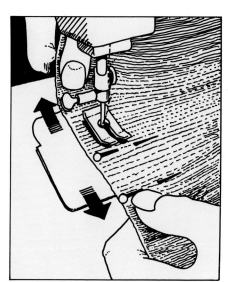

5 Stretching ribbing in place as you stitch

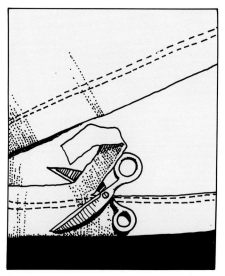

6 Trimming away excess fabric after stitching hem

Out and About

This chapter features clothes that look like a million dollars but don't cost it. These days we all like our clothes to be easy – easy to wear and look after – and adaptable for many occasions. The smart styles in this chapter look equally good at work, for a day out in town, a movie or a casual dinner with friends. These clothes are as versatile as today's woman and just as smart!

You will also find that these clothes, made in easy-care stretch fabrics, need very little looking after. Simply wash, gently pull back into shape and drip-dry and they are all set to go again and again.

Add a smart scarf, some wonderful earrings or even a hat and these outfits will carry you just about anywhere.

SWEATSHIRT

SIZE: 12/14

MATERIALS

- ☐ **1.30 m of 140 cm wide fleecy knit fabric**
- ☐ **40 cm of 80 cm wide ribbing**
- ☐ **purchased knitted collar**
- ☐ **50 cm narrow stay-tape for shoulder seams**

PATTERN

See Pattern 5 (long sleeve)
Cut ribbing as follows:
Neck, 8 cm long x 36 cm wide. Hipband, 14 cm long x 80 cm wide. Cuffs, two 14 cm long x 20 cm wide.
Front (cut 1), Back (cut 1), Sleeve (cut 2).
Cut out pattern pieces as directed. 1 cm seams allowed. Join all pieces together with right sides facing. Exposed raw edges can be neatened by overlocking, zigzagging, or simply left raw, as knit fabric will not fray.

TO MAKE

1   Stitch shoulder seams, attaching stay-tape as you sew. Press. Stitch sleeves to body around armholes, matching notches. Press.
2   Stitch front to back along underarm seams, matching underarm points. Press.
3   Stitch short edges of neck ribbing to form tube. Fold in half with seams inside. Place evenly around neck with raw edges matching, and ribbing seam at centre back. Then place purchased collar, with opening at centre front, on top of ribbing and pin through all layers. You may prefer to tack this seam before stitching. Stitch with overlocking or zigzagging so that neck opening will stretch sufficiently. Press seam away from ribbing.
4   Make cuff ribbing as neck ribbing. Pin evenly around sleeve ends with raw edges and seams matching. Stitch and press as for neck ribbing. Repeat for hipband.

SHORT CIRCULAR SKIRT

SIZE: 10/12

MATERIALS

- ☐ **1.60 m of 150 cm wide cotton knit**
- ☐ **20 cm of 70 cm wide ribbing**
- ☐ **70 cm of 2 cm wide elastic**

PATTERN

See Pattern 2 (pocket only) on page 71
Cut waistband ribbing 20 cm long x 66 cm wide.
Draw quarter-circle for skirt pattern as follows:
1   Draw square on paper 70 cm x 70 cm.
2   From the point of one corner, with a radius of 13 cm, draw a small quarter-circle (for quarter-waist seam of 21 cm).
3   From the same point, radius 70 cm, draw a large quarter-circle for skirt hem.
4   Mark one straight edge with 'centre front/centre back, place on fold', and the other straight edge with 'side seam, place along straight grain of fabric'. Label pattern piece with 'front/back circular skirt. Cut 1 front and 1 back both on fold'.
5   Mark notches for pocket opening on side seam, 4 cm and 20 cm down from waist.
Front Skirt (cut 1), Back Skirt (cut 1), Pocket (cut 4).

Cut out pattern pieces as directed. 1 cm seams and 2 cm hem allowed. Join all pieces together with right sides facing. Exposed raw edges can be neatened by overlocking, zigzagging, or simply left raw, as knit fabric will not fray.

TO MAKE

1   Stitch long straight edge of pockets to side seams, matching notches. Press.
2   Just inside pocket seam, stitch side seams of skirt from waist down to upper notch. Just inside pocket seam, stitch side seams from lower notch down to hem. Stitch curved edges of pockets together. Press.
3   Stitch short edges of ribbing to form tube. Fold in half with seams inside. Stitch elastic ends to fit waist, and insert inside ribbing waistband. Mark lower edge of waistband and skirt waist into quarters. Pin waistband evenly around waist on top of skirt, matching markings, and with ribbing seam at centre back. Stitch. Press seam away from ribbing.
4   Allow skirt to hang for a week before levelling hem to suit, allowing a 2 cm hem. Press under and topstitch and edgestitch to finish.

HINT

When hanging a circular skirt for the hem to drop, be sure the waist is held horizontally. Pinning the skirt by the waist to the back of curtains is a good out-of-the-way place to achieve this.

HOW TO APPLIQUE STRETCH FABRICS

Colourful appliques are a delight-ful way to decorate any garment, and they're surprisingly easy to do. You will need a machine that zigzags, some simple haberdash-ery items, and one other thing – your imagination! An effective applique can give new life to an old favourite, dress up the basic sweatshirt, trim a pocket or even hide that stain or tear you'd like to disappear.

You can purchase ready-to-stitch appliques at fabric shops, or be creative and make your own from the motifs that your printed fabric presents. Decide which motif will be decorative, cut it out leaving 1 cm around the design itself. Reinforce the back of the motif with lightweight iron-on in-terfacing and apply the same in-terfacing to the back of the fabric to be appliqued. The interfacing will hold the fabric firmly and not allow it to 'stretch' out of shape while you're stitching around it.

*Pin the motif into position, turn your machine to a medium width zigzag stitch and sew around the motif outline. Carefully trim away the excess fabric beyond the stitching. Now turn your machine to a wider, closer satin stitch, and stitch again **over** the zigzag stitch-ing, covering the cut edge of the motif.*

When you become confident with your ability to applique, try padding the motif lightly with thin quilting wadding, and highlighting areas of the motif with stitching, perhaps even with gold or silver sewing thread!

By adding several motifs a whole picture can be built up on skirts and fronts and backs of sweat shirts. Remember, you are only limited by your imagination!

NARROW PANTS

SIZE: 10/12

MATERIALS
- ☐ **1.20 m of 140 cm wide cotton knit fabric**
- ☐ **70 cm of 2 cm wide elastic**

PATTERN
See Pattern 4

Front and Back Leg (cut 2).

Cut out pattern piece as directed. 1 cm seams and 2 cm hems allowed. Join all pieces together with right sides facing. 3 cm turning allowed at waist. Exposed raw edges can be neatened by overlocking, zigzagging, or simply left raw, as knit fabric will not fray.

TO MAKE
1   Stitch inside leg seam on each leg. Press. Stitch crotch seam, matching fronts, backs and inside leg points. Press.

3   To form casing for elastic, turn under 3 cm at waist edge. Press. Stitch around waist 2.5 cm from edge leaving gap at centre back for inserting elastic. Cut elastic to fit waist, insert and join ends. Stitch gap closed.

4   Turn hems up to suit. Press. Topstitch and edgestitch to finish.

DOLMAN SLEEVED TUNIC

SIZE: 10/12/14

MATERIALS
- ☐ **1.80 m of 140 cm wide fleecy knit fabric**
- ☐ **30 cm of 140 cm wide contrast print fleecy knit fabric**
- ☐ **15 cm nylon zipper**
- ☐ **shoulder pads**

PATTERN
See Pattern 3 (short length)

Cut contrast fabric bands as follows:
Piping, four 5 cm long x 80 cm wide.
Collar, 8 cm long x 40 cm wide. Cuffs, two 8 cm long x 20 cm wide.

Centre Front (cut 1), Centre Back (cut 2), Side Front (cut 2), Side Back (cut 2).

Cut out pattern pieces as directed. 1 cm seams and 2 cm hem allowed. Join all pieces together with right sides facing. Exposed raw edges can be neatened by overlocking, zigzagging, or simply left raw, as knit fabric will not fray.

TO MAKE

1   Press piping strips over double, wrong sides facing. Tack evenly to vertical seams of centre front and centre back pieces, matching raw edges. Pin centre front to side fronts. Stitch through all thicknesses, catching piping as you sew. Press seams to centre and piping to side. Repeat for back pieces.

2   Pin shoulder seams evenly from neck to cuff, matching piping positions. Stitch. Press. Pin underarm seams evenly from hem to cuff. Stitch. Press.

3   Stitch centre back seam from notch at bottom of zipper down to hem. Press.

4   Press collar over double, wrong sides facing. Press. Pin evenly around neck, matching raw edges. Stitch. Press seam away from collar. Press under 1 cm at back neck opening. Pin zipper in place from top of collar, turning zipper ends under to neaten. Stitch.

5   Stitch short ends of cuff to form tube. Fold in half with seams inside. Pin evenly around sleeve ends with raw edges and seams matching. Stitch. Press seam away from cuff. Repeat for other cuff.

6   Turn hem under to suit. Press. Trim to 2 cm. Topstitch and edgestitch to finish.

DOLMAN SLEEVED DRESS

SIZE: 10/12/14

MATERIALS

☐ **2.50 m of 140 cm wide fleecy knit fabric**
☐ **30 cm of 90 cm wide ribbing**
☐ **15 cm nylon zipper**
☐ **shoulder pads**

PATTERN

See Pattern 3 (long length)
Cut ribbing as follows:
Piping, four 3 cm long x 90 cm wide.
Collar, 8 cm long x 38 cm wide. Cuffs, two 8 cm long x 18 cm wide.
Centre Front (cut 1), Centre Back (cut 2)
Side Front (cut 2) Side Back (cut 2).
Cut out pattern pieces as directed. 1 cm seams and 2 cm hem allowed. Join all pieces together with right sides facing. Exposed raw edges can be neatened by overlocking, zigzagging, or simply left raw, as knit fabric will not fray.

TO MAKE

As for DOLMAN SLEEVED TUNIC on page 12. Ribbing is used for piping, collar and cuffs instead of contrast print, but the making process is the same.

CARDIGAN JACKET

SIZE: 12/14

MATERIALS

- ☐ **1.50 m of 140 cm wide fleecy knit fabric**
- ☐ **70 cm of 84 cm wide ribbing**
- ☐ **six 2 cm self-colour buttons**
- ☐ **40 cm narrow stay-tape for shoulder seams**
- ☐ **shoulder pads**

PATTERN

See Pattern 1
Cut ribbing as follows:
Neck and Front Band, two 10 cm long x 75 cm wide. Hipband, 18 cm long x 84 cm wide. Cuffs, two 18 cm long x 18 cm wide. Pocket Band, two 10 cm long x 19 cm wide.
For pockets, cut two rectangles in fleecy knit 19 cm long x 21 cm wide.
Front (cut 2), Back (cut 1), Sleeve (cut 2). Cut out pattern pieces as directed. 1 cm seams allowed. Join all pieces together with right sides facing. Exposed raw edges can be neatened by overlocking, zigzagging, or simply left raw, as knit fabric will not fray.

TO MAKE

1 Fold pocket ribbing in half along width. Pin evenly to pocket top, with right sides facing and matching raw edges. Stitch. Press seams away from ribbing. Fold under 1 cm at front edge of pocket. Press. Place

HINT

Children can grow out of clothes almost overnight, it seems! Often this growth is in length only. It's easy to insert lengthening bands of fabric in a contrasting colour.

Unpick the underarm, side or leg seams 10 cm more than the width of the lengthening band. Cut straight across the arm, leg or bodice through the centre of this opening. Sew in the lengthening band, then restitch the unpicked seams.

Try to use similar weight fabric as the garment for the bands.

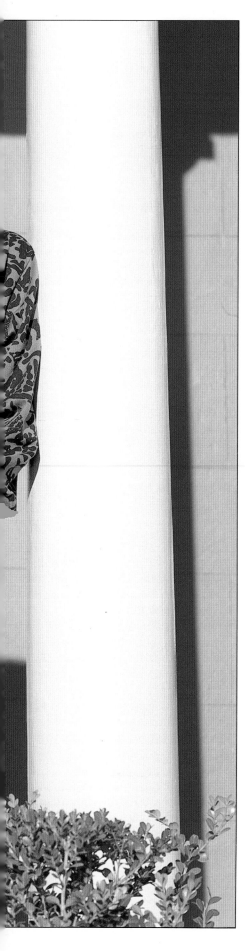

pocket on jacket front so that raw edges at side seam and hem match. Pin then stitch pocket front to jacket, from inside the folded edge. Repeat for other pocket.

2   Stitch shoulder seams, attaching stay-tape as you sew. Press. Stitch sleeves to body around armholes, matching notches. Press.

3   Stitch front to back along underarm seams, matching underarm points, and catching pockets into side seams as you go. Press.

4   Stitch short ends of cuff ribbing to form tube. Fold in half with seams inside. Pin evenly around sleeve ends with raw edges and seams matching. Stitch with over-locking or zigzagging so that cuff seam will stretch sufficiently. Press seam away from ribbing.

5   Fold hipband ribbing in half, pin evenly around jacket hem with raw edges matching, from centre front to other centre front. Stitch. Press seam away from ribbing.

6   To make neck and front band, stitch ribbing pieces together along one short edge for centre back seam. With right sides facing, fold other short ends in half and stitch to form bottom edge. Turn to right side and fold in half, pin around front and neck edge of jacket, from hem to hem. Stitch. Press seam away from ribbing.

7   To position buttonholes on right front band, mark centre of lower one 2 cm from finished jacket hem. Mark five more up from lower one with 10 cm spacing between each centre. Make buttonholes (see hint). Stitch buttons on left front band.

8   Position shoulder pads to suit and stitch in place.

EIGHT GORE SKIRT

SIZE: 10/12

MATERIALS
- [ ] **2.40 m of 150 cm wide cotton knit fabric**
- [ ] **70 cm of 2 cm wide elastic**

PATTERN
See Pattern 6
Skirt (cut 8).
Cut out pattern pieces as directed. 1 cm seams and 2 cm hem allowed. Join all pieces together with right sides facing. Exposed raw edges can be neatened by overlocking, zigzagging, or simply left raw, as knit fabric will not fray.

TO MAKE
1   Stitch all eight panels together along vertical seams. Press.

2   To form casing for elastic, turn under 3 cm at waist edge. Press. Stitch around waist 2.5 cm from edge, leaving gap at centre back for inserting elastic. Cut elastic to fit waist, insert and join ends. Stitch gap closed.

3   Turn hem up to suit. Press. Trim to 2 cm. Blindstitch or topstitch and edgestitch hem to finish.

WRAP-AROUND TOP

SIZE: 10/12/14

MATERIALS
- [ ] **1.20 m of 150 cm wide cotton knit fabric**
- [ ] **50 cm narrow stay-tape for shoulder seams**

PATTERN
See Pattern 7
Front (cut 2), Back (cut 1), Sleeve (cut 2), Tie (cut 2).
Cut out pattern pieces as directed. 1 cm seams and 2 cm hems and edges allowed. Join all pieces together with right sides facing. Exposed raw edges can be neatened by overlocking, zigzagging, or simply left raw, as knit fabric will not fray.

TO MAKE
1   Stitch shoulder seams, attaching stay-tape as you sew. Press. Stitch sleeves to body around armholes, matching notches. Press.

2   Stitch front to back along underarm seams, matching underarm points. Press. Stitch ties to fronts, matching notches. Press.

3   Turn under 1 cm on lower edge of sleeves. Press. Turn under 1 cm again. Press. Topstitch and edgestitch to finish. Repeat process around entire edge of garment.

HINT

If you need to make buttonholes on stretch garments, reinforce the fabric at the back of the buttonhole position with some iron-on interfacing, and satin stitch over a length of thread. This will help prevent the stitching curling and becoming warped.

WRAP-AROUND TOP

SIZE: 10/12/14

MATERIALS
- ☐ **1.20 m of 150 cm wide cotton knit fabric**
- ☐ **50 cm narrow stay-tape for shoulder seams**

PATTERN
See Pattern 7
Front (cut 2), Back (cut 1), Sleeve (cut 2), Tie (cut 2).
Cut out pattern pieces as directed. 1 cm seams and 2 cm hems and edges allowed. Join all pieces together with right sides facing. Exposed raw edges can be neatened by overlocking, zigzagging, or simply left raw, as knit fabric will not fray.

TO MAKE
1 Stitch shoulder seams, attaching stay-tape as you sew. Press. Stitch sleeves to body around armholes, matching notches. Press.
2 Stitch front to back along underarm seams, matching underarm points. Press. Stitch ties to fronts, matching notches. Press.

FABRIC CONVERSION CHART

This chart will help you to solve problems which occur when the width of fabric chosen is not the same as in the pattern instructions.
How To Use the Chart
A pattern calls for 2.10 m of 140 cm wide fabric but the fabric you have chosen is 115 cm wide. Read down the 140 cm column until you find 2.10. Then read across the line on which 2.10 appears until you reach the 115 cm column. The number in this column is the amount of 115 cm fabric to buy: 2.55 m of 115 cm wide fabric.

We suggest that you purchase an additional 30 cm of fabric if using: a pattern that includes nap or one-way directional printed fabrics; sleeves cut in one with the body of the garment; and pants and pant-suits, especially if buying fabric narrower than specified.

3   Turn under 1 cm on lower edge of sleeves. Press. Turn under 1 cm again. Press. Topstitch and edgestitch to finish. Repeat process around entire edge of garment.

GATHERED PANTS

SIZE: 10/12/14

MATERIALS
☐ **1.50 m of 150 cm wide cotton knit fabric**
☐ **70 cm of 2 cm wide elastic**

PATTERN
See Pattern 8 (long length)
Front (cut 2), Back (cut 2), Pocket (cut 4). Cut out pattern pieces as directed. 1 cm seams and 2 cm hem allowed. Join all pieces together with right sides facing. Exposed raw edges can be neatened by overlocking, zigzagging, or simply left raw, as knit fabric will not fray.

TO MAKE
1   Stitch long straight edge of pockets to side seams, matching notches. Press.
2   Just inside pocket seam, stitch side seams of pants from waist down to upper notch. Just inside pocket seam, stitch side seams from lower notch down to hem. Stitch curved edges of pockets together. Press.
3   Stitch inside leg seams. Press. Stitch around crotch seam from front waist to back waist, matching inside leg seam points. Press.
4   To form casing for elastic, turn under 3 cm at waist edge. Press. Stitch around waist 2.5 cm from edge leaving gap at centre back for inserting elastic. Cut elastic to fit waist, insert and join ends. Stitch gap closed.
5   Turn hem up to suit. Press. Trim to 2 cm. Topstitch and edgestitch to finish.

HINT

Pregnant? Stretch clothes are just perfect for you now. Not only are they comfortable, but they can grow along with your expanding shape! These Gathered Pants will be really useful. Don't bother to stitch closed the gap for the waist elastic, that way you can keep inserting longer elastic as the months pass. The same goes for the Drawstring Shorts on page 32 using the same pattern.

Even more useful and flattering –

as they will give you super slim legs to balance that growing waistline – are the Narrow Pants on page 12. Our fashion designer wore them right through to the ninth month, ending up with a comfortable 95 cm of elastic at the waist! Make several pairs in your basic colours and they can go under all your favourite baggy tops and sweaters. Who needs maternity clothes?

Fabric Widths			
90 cm	115 cm	140 cm	150 cm
metre	metre	metre	metre
1.60	1.30	1.05	0.95
1.85	1.50	1.30	1.15
2.10	1.60	1.40	1.30
2.30	1.95	1.60	1.50
2.65	2.10	1.75	1.60
2.90	2.30	1.85	1.75
3.10	2.55	2.10	1.85
3.45	2.65	2.20	2.10
4.15	3.10	2.55	2.40
4.35	3.35	2.65	2.55
4.60	3.55	2.90	2.65

Active Kids

We all look for no-fuss clothes for babies, tots and the 'just-at-school' kids which wash well and keep bouncing back – just like their owners! These patterns are sized for little ones of six months, four years and six years of age. For a two year old, check out the great tracksuit in the 'Ready for Bed' chapter beginning on page 44.

The clothes in this section are designed to be sturdy as well as stylish. Choose your materials and colours well, add a little extra fabric in the hems and seams, and they could suit several children over the years, without that well-worn, hand-me-down look.

For some extra tips on adapting pattern sizes for different ages, make sure you read the 'How To' section on page 50.

V-NECK T-SHIRT

SIZE: Age 6 years

MATERIALS
- ☐ **50 cm of 150 cm wide cotton knit fabric**
- ☐ **20 cm long x 25 cm wide piece of contrast cotton knit fabric for V-neck.**
- ☐ **10 cm long x 40 cm wide ribbing**
- ☐ **50 cm narrow stay-tape for shoulder seams**

PATTERN
See Pattern 9 (with V-neck)
Cut Neck Ribbing, 8 cm long x 34 cm wide.
V Section (cut 1 contrast), Front (cut 1), Back (cut 1), Sleeve (cut 2).
Cut out pattern pieces as directed. 1 cm seams and 2 cm hems allowed. Join all pieces together with right sides facing.

Exposed raw edges can be neatened by overlocking, zigzagging, or simply left raw, as knit fabric will not fray.

TO MAKE
1 Pin V section to front, matching centre front points and raw edges. Stitch, snipping centre front point almost to stitching so you can stitch around the V. Press seam away from V section. Topstitch and edgestitch to finish.
2 Stitch shoulder seams, attaching stay-tape as you sew. Press. Stitch sleeves to body around armholes, matching notches. Press. Stitch front to back along underarm seams, matching underarm points. Press.
3 Stitch short edges of neck ribbing to form tube. Fold in half with seams inside. Pin evenly around neck with raw edges matching, and ribbing seam at centre back. Stitch with overlocking or zigzagging so that neck opening will stretch sufficiently.

Press seam away from ribbing.
4 Turn under 2 cm at sleeve end. Press. Topstitch and edgestitch to finish. Repeat for hem.

SHORTS

SIZE: Age 6 years

MATERIALS
- ☐ **50 cm of 150 cm wide cotton knit fabric**
- ☐ **60 cm of 2 cm wide elastic**

PATTERN
See Pattern 10 (straight hems)
Front (cut 2), Back (cut 2), Pocket (cut 4).
Cut out pattern pieces as directed. 1 cm seams and 2 cm hems allowed. Join all pieces together with right sides facing. Exposed raw edges can be neatened by

overlocking, zigzagging, or simply left raw, as knit fabric will not fray.

TO MAKE

1 Stitch long straight edge of pockets to side seams, matching notches. Press.

2 Just inside pocket seam, stitch side seams of pants from waist down to upper notch. Just inside pocket seam, stitch side seams from lower notch down to hem. Press. Stitch curved edges of pockets together, then topstitch and edgestitch through to right side of shorts to hold in place.

3 Stitch inside leg seams. Press. Stitch around crotch seam from front waist to back waist, matching inside leg seam points. Press.

4 To form casing for elastic, turn under 3 cm at waist edge. Press. Stitch around waist 2.5 cm from edge, leaving gap at centre back for inserting elastic. Cut elastic to fit waist, insert and join ends. Stitch gap closed.

5 Turn hem up to suit. Press. Trim to 2 cm. Topstitch and edgestitch to finish.

T-SHIRT

SIZE: Age 6 years

MATERIALS

☐ **50 cm of 150 cm wide cotton knit fabric**
☐ **30 cm of 80 cm wide ribbing**
☐ **50 cm narrow stay-tape for shoulder seams**

PATTERN

See Pattern 9 (shorter sleeve)
Cut ribbing as follows:
Neck, 8 cm long x 34 cm wide. Hipband, 12 cm long x 64 cm wide. Cuffs, two 8 cm long x 32 cm wide. Front (cut 1), Back (cut 1), Sleeve (cut 2).
Cut out pattern pieces as directed. 1 cm seams allowed. Join all pieces together

with right sides facing. Note that exposed raw edges can be neatened by overlocking, zigzagging, or simply left raw, as knit fabric will not fray.

TO MAKE

1 Stitch shoulder seams, attaching stay-tape as you sew. Press. Stitch sleeves to body around armholes, matching notches. Press. Stitch front to back along underarm and side seams, matching underarm points. Press.

2 Stitch short edges of neck ribbing to form tube. Fold in half with seams inside. Pin evenly around neck with raw edges matching, and ribbing seam at centre back. Stitch with overlocking or zigzagging so that neck opening will stretch sufficiently. Press seam away from ribbing.

3 Make cuff ribbing as neck ribbing. Pin evenly around sleeve ends with raw edges and seams matching. Stitch and press as for neck ribbing. Repeat for hipband.

HINT

Cut often-used patterns out of firm non-adhesive interfacing. They will last much longer and not become tattered and torn.

Any markings on the pattern, such as grain lines, can be easily transferred.

TRACKSUIT

SIZE: Age 6 months

MATERIALS

- ☐ **80 cm of 130 cm wide fleecy knit fabric**
- ☐ **30 cm of 80 cm wide ribbing**
- ☐ **50 cm of 2 cm wide elastic**

PATTERN

See Pattern 11
Cut ribbing as follows:
Neck, 6 cm long x 28 cm wide. Hipband, 10 cm long x 50 cm wide. Cuffs, two 10 cm long x 12 cm wide. Ankles, two 10 cm long x 15 cm wide. Piping, cut two 3 cm strips across width of ribbing, to give you four 20 cm strips for armholes and two 40 cm strips for legs.
Front Body (cut 1), Back Body (cut 1), Sleeve (cut 2), Front Leg (cut 2), Back Leg (cut 2).
Cut out pattern pieces as directed. 1 cm seams allowed. Join all pieces together with right sides facing. Exposed raw edges can be neatened by overlocking, zigzagging, or simply left raw, as knit fabric will not fray.

TO MAKE

Top:
1 Press piping strips over double, wrong sides facing. Tack armhole piping strips to right side of all four raglan armhole edges. Pin sleeves to armholes. Stitch through all thicknesses, catching piping as you sew. Press seams away from sleeves.
2 Stitch front to back along underarm seams, matching underarm points. Press.
3 Stitch short edges of neck ribbing to form tube. Fold in half with seams inside. Pin evenly around neck with raw edges matching, and ribbing seam at centre back. Stitch with overlocking or zigzagging so that neck opening will stretch sufficiently. Press seam away from ribbing.
4 Make cuff ribbing as neck ribbing. Pin evenly around sleeve ends with raw edges and seams matching. Stitch and press as for neck ribbing. Repeat for hipband.
Pants:
5 Tack leg piping strips to right side of front leg side seam edges. Pin back legs on top. Stitch through all thicknesses, catching piping as you sew. Press seams to front and piping to back.
6 Stitch inside leg seams. Press. Stitch around crotch seam from front waist to back waist, matching inside leg seam points. Press.
7 To form casing for elastic, turn under 3 cm at waist edge. Press. Stitch around waist 2.5 cm from edge, leaving gap at centre back for inserting elastic. Cut elastic to fit waist, insert and join ends. Stitch gap closed.
8 Make ankle ribbing as neck ribbing. Pin evenly around leg ends with raw edges and seams matching. Stitch. Press seams away from ribbing.

HINT

Test for correct foot pressure on any bulky fabric you sew. Remember that some brushed knit fabrics are thicker than usual, and may be difficult to pass underneath the machine foot. You may also like to increase your stitch length to make sewing smoother.

VEST and PANTS

SIZE: Age 6 months

MATERIALS
- ☐ **50 cm of 140 cm wide cotton knit fabric**
- ☐ **1.10 m of 1 cm wide elastic**

PATTERN
See Pattern 12
Front (cut 1), Back (cut 1), Sleeve (cut 2), Front and Back Leg (cut 2).
Cut out pattern pieces as directed. 1 cm seams and 2 cm hems and edges allowed. Join all pieces together with right sides facing. Exposed raw edges can be neatened by overlocking, zigzagging, or simply left raw, as knit fabric will not fray.

TO MAKE
Top:
1 Turn under 2 cm at neck edges. Press. Topstitch and edgestitch to finish.

2 Lay back neck over front neck, matching notches at armhole edges. Stitch sleeves to body around armholes, matching notches. Press. Stitch front to back along underarm seams and down side seams, matching underarm points. Press.
3 Turn sleeve ends under 2 cm. Press. Topstitch and edgestitch to finish. Repeat for hem.
Pants:
4 Stitch inside leg seams. Press. Stitch around crotch seam from front waist to back waist, matching inside leg seam points. Press.
5 To form casing for elastic, turn under 2 cm at waist edge. Press. Stitch around waist 1.5 cm from edge, leaving gap at centre back for inserting elastic. Cut elastic to fit waist, insert and join ends. Stitch gap closed. Repeat for leg elastic.

NOTE: This simple vest works just as well as a T-shirt.

SLEEPSUIT

SIZE: Age 6 months

MATERIALS
- ☐ **1.20 cm of 120 cm wide cotton knit fabric**
- ☐ **45 cm nylon zipper**
- ☐ **20 cm narrow elastic**

PATTERN
See Pattern 13
For piping, cut fabric into 3 cm wide strips on the bias as follows:
50 cm long for collar edge, two 20 cm long for cuffs, four 20 cm long for armholes, 40 cm long for inside neck binding, 40 cm long for bow (optional).
Right Front (cut 1), Left Front (cut 1), Left Front Extension (cut 1), Back (cut 2), Sleeve (cut 2), Collar (cut 2).
Cut out pattern pieces as directed. 1 cm seams allowed. Join all pieces together with right sides facing. Exposed raw edges can be neatened by overlocking, zigzagging, or simply left raw, as knit fabric will not fray.

TO MAKE
1 Stitch right front to left front extension from crotch point to A, matching raw edges. Stitch left front to left front extension from foot to B. Press seams.
2 Press in seam allowances on front opening. Sew zipper into place beneath pressed edges with pull tab 1.5 cm below neck edge.
3 Make pleats on outside of both back foot sections as marked. Stitch centre back seam. Press.

4   Press bias strips over double, wrong sides facing. Tack armhole bias strips to right side of all four raglan armhole edges. Pin sleeves to armholes. Stitch through all thicknesses, catching bias as you sew. Press seams away from sleeves.

5   Tack folded collar bias strip around outside edge of right side of one collar section, keeping raw edges even. Place two collar sections together with right sides facing. Stitch around outside edge. Trim seams. Turn and press.

6   Tack collar around neck edge, clipping neck edge if necessary, and keeping raw edges even. Pin bias strip around neck edge over collar seam, with right sides facing and raw edges even. Stitch. Turn bias to inside. Turn under all raw edges and stitch down. Press.

7   Stitch cuff bias strips around sleeve ends with raw edges even. Turn raw edges to inside and stitch down, forming casing. Press. Thread narrow elastic through casing. Secure ends of elastic.

8   Sew front to back, stitching in one continuous seam from sleeve end around legs to sleeve end, matching underarm and crotch points. Press.

9   To make tie for optional bow, fold bias strip in half along length, right sides facing. Sew across one end and down the length. Trim seams close to stitching. Turn to right side. Knot ends tightly, trim. Stitch very securely at neck and tie bow.

COLOUR BLOCK TRACKSUIT

SIZE: Age 4 years

MATERIALS

- [ ] **90 cm of 160 cm wide red fleecy knit fabric**
- [ ] **20 cm of 50 cm wide blue fleecy knit fabric**
- [ ] **20 cm of 50 cm wide yellow fleecy knit fabric**
- [ ] **30 cm of 90 cm wide green ribbing**
- [ ] **30 cm narrow stay-tape for shoulder seams**
- [ ] **60 cm of 2 cm wide elastic**

PATTERN

See Pattern 14
Cut green ribbing as follows:
Neck, 8 cm long x 34 cm wide. Hipband, 12 cm long x 58 cm wide. Cuffs, two 12 cm long x 14 cm wide. Ankles, two 12 cm long x 20 cm wide.
Upper Right Front (cut 1 yellow), Upper Left Front (cut 1 red), Lower Right Front (cut 1 red), Lower Left Front (cut 1 blue), Upper Right Back (cut 1 red), Upper Left Back (cut 1 yellow), Lower Right Back (cut 1 blue), Lower Left Back (cut 1 red), Sleeve (cut 2 red), Front and Back Leg (cut 2 red). Cut out pattern pieces as directed. 1 cm seams allowed. Join all pieces together with right sides facing. Exposed raw edges can be neatened by overlocking, zigzagging, or simply left raw, as knit fabric will not fray.

TO MAKE

Top:
1   Stitch coloured body pieces together to make complete front and back. Press. Stitch shoulder seams, attaching stay-tape as you sew.
2   Stitch sleeves to body along armhole seams, matching notches. Stitch front to back along underarm and side seams, matching underarm points. Press.
3   Stitch short edges of neck ribbing to form tube. Fold in half with seams inside. Pin evenly around neck with raw edges matching, and ribbing seam at centre back. Stitch with overlocking or zigzagging so that neck opening will stretch sufficiently. Press seam away from ribbing.
4   Make cuff ribbing as neck ribbing. Pin evenly around sleeve ends with raw edges and seams matching. Stitch and press as for neck ribbing. Repeat for hipband.
Pants:
5   Stitch inside leg seams. Press. Stitch

Front Leg (cut 2), Back Leg (cut 2).
Cut out pattern pieces as directed. 1 cm seams allowed. Join all pieces together with right sides facing. Exposed raw edges can be neatened by overlocking, zigzagging, or simply left raw, as knit fabric will not fray.

TO MAKE

Top:

1   Press piping strips over double, wrong sides facing. Tack armhole piping strips to right side of all four raglan armhole edges. Pin sleeves to armholes. Stitch through all thicknesses, catching piping as you go. Press seams away from sleeves.

2   Stitch front to back along underarm seams, matching underarm points. Press.

3   Stitch short edges of neck ribbing to form tube. Fold in half with seams inside. Pin evenly around neck with raw edges matching, and ribbing seam at centre back. Stitch with overlocking or zigzagging so that neck opening will stretch sufficiently. Press seam away from ribbing.

4   Make cuff ribbing as neck ribbing. Pin evenly around sleeve ends with raw edges and sleeves matching. Stitch and press as for neck ribbing. Repeat for hipband.

Pants:

5   Tack leg piping strips to right side of front leg side seam edges. Pin back legs on top. Stitch through all thicknesses, catching piping as you sew. Press seams to front and piping to back.

6   Stitch inside leg seams. Press. Stitch around crotch seam from front waist to back waist, matching inside leg seam points. Press.

around crotch seam from front waist to back waist, matching inside leg seam points. Press.

6   To form casing for elastic, turn under 3 cm at waist edge. Press. Stitch around waist 2.5 cm from edge, leaving gap at centre back for inserting elastic. Cut elastic to fit waist, insert and join ends. Stitch gap closed.

7   Make ankle ribbing as neck ribbing. Pin evenly around leg ends with raw edges and seams matching. Stitch. Press seams away from ribbing.

PATTERN

See Pattern 11
Cut ribbing as follows:
Neck, 6 cm long x 28 cm wide blue.
Hipband, 10 cm long x 50 cm wide red.
Cuffs, two 10 cm long x 12 cm wide green.
Ankles, two 10 cm long x 15 cm wide blue.
Piping, cut two 3 cm strips across width of yellow ribbing, to give you four 20 cm strips for armholes and two 40 cm strips for legs.
Front Body (cut 1), Back Body (cut 1), Sleeve (cut 2),

7   To form casing for elastic, turn under 3 cm at waist edge. Press. Stitch around waist 2.5 cm from edge, leaving gap at centre back for inserting elastic. Cut elastic to fit waist, insert and join ends. Stitch gap closed.

8 Make ankle ribbing as neck ribbing. Pin evenly around leg ends with raw edges and seams matching. Stitch. Press seams away from ribbing.

TRACKSUIT

SIZE: Age 6 months

MATERIALS

☐ **80 cm of 130 cm wide stretch towelling print fabric**
☐ **10 cm long x 80 cm wide yellow ribbing**
☐ **10 cm long x 60 cm wide blue ribbing**
☐ **10 cm long x 30 cm wide green ribbing**
☐ **10 cm long x 50 cm wide red ribbing**
☐ **50 cm of 2 cm wide elastic**

Beach Sports

O nce summer days arrive, everyone eagerly
tosses aside the winter clothes in favour of loose
T-shirts, singlet dresses, voluminous shorts —
all the gear that spells fun and relaxation.

These clothes are so straightforward you can
actually have fun and relax making them! Make sure
you choose bold and splashy fabrics for the various
shorts, T-shirts, swimsuits and so on. Summer is no time
for muted shades. And make sure you look over our next
chapter on holiday wear, because the sarongs, skirts and
wrap-over tops are ideal for dressing up these more
casual pieces.

This chapter will have the whole family dressed
stylishly in cool stretch fabrics like cotton interlock before
you can say 'Sun's up!'.

T-SHIRT

SIZE: M/L Man

MATERIALS
- ☐ **1.10 m of 150 cm wide cotton knit fabric**
- ☐ **10 cm of 40 cm wide ribbing**
- ☐ **50 cm narrow stay-tape for shoulder seams**
- ☐ **scrap of contrast print cotton knit fabric for applique**

PATTERN
See Pattern 15 (short sleeve)
Neck band, cut 6 cm long x 38 cm wide of ribbing. Pocket, cut 18 cm x 18 cm square of cotton knit fabric.
Front (cut 1), Back (cut 1), Sleeve (cut 2). Cut out pattern pieces as directed. 1 cm seams and 2 cm hems allowed. Join all pieces together with right sides facing. Exposed raw edges can be neatened by overlocking, zigzagging, or simply left raw, as knit fabric will not fray.

TO MAKE
1 Turn under 2 cm at pocket top edge. Press. Topstitch and edgestitch to finish. Turn under 1 cm at sides and lower edge. Press.
2 Decide which motif from your contrast print you want to applique. Carefully cut out, allowing 6 mm allowance from your intended stitching line. Place motif carefully onto pocket in desired position. Pin securely.
3 Using a small machine stitch, sew motif to pocket around stitching line. Trim fabric away very close to stitching. Using narrow, closely-spaced zigzag, stitch over first stitching line to cover raw edge. Press. We suggest you practise a test applique first with some spare fabrics.
4 Pin pocket to front on left side. Topstitch and edgestitch in place.
5 Stitch shoulder seams, attaching staytape as you sew. Press. Stitch sleeves to body around armholes, matching notches. Press. Stitch front to back along underarm seams, matching underarm points. Press seams towards back.
6 Stitch short edges of neck ribbing to form tube. Fold in half with seams inside. Pin evenly around neck with raw edges matching, and ribbing seam at centre back. Stitch with overlocking or zigzagging so that neck opening will stretch sufficiently. Press seam away from ribbing.
7 Turn under 2 cm at sleeve hem. Press. Topstitch and edgestitch to finish. Turn hem up to suit. Press. Trim to 2 cm. Topstitch and edgestitch to finish.

EASY SHORTS

SIZE: M/L Man

MATERIALS
- ☐ **1 m of 150 cm wide cotton knit fabric**
- ☐ **90 cm of 2 cm wide elastic**

PATTERN
See Pattern 16 (medium length)
Front (cut 2), Back (cut 2), Pocket (cut 4). Cut out pattern pieces as directed. 1 cm seams and 2 cm hem allowed. Join all pieces together with right sides facing. Exposed raw edges can be neatened by overlocking, zigzagging, or simply left raw, as knit fabric will not fray.

TO MAKE
1 Stitch long straight edge of pockets to side seams, matching notches. Press.
2 Just inside pocket seam, stitch side seams of pants from waist down to upper notch. Just inside pocket seam, stitch side seams from lower notch down to hem. Stitch curved edges of pockets together. Press.
3 Stitch inside leg seams. Press. Stitch around crotch seam from front waist to back waist, matching inside leg seam points. Press.
4 To form casing for elastic, turn under 3 cm at waist edge. Press. Stitch around waist 2.5 cm from edge, leaving gap at centre back for inserting elastic. Cut elastic to fit waist, insert and join ends. Stitch gap closed.
5 Turn hem up to suit. Press. Trim to 2 cm. Topstitch and edgestitch to finish.

SINGLET

SIZE: M/L Man

MATERIALS

- **80 cm of 150 cm wide cotton knit fabric**
- **scraps of contrast print cotton knit fabric for applique (see "How to applique" box on page 11)**

PATTERN

See Pattern 17
Front (cut 1), Back (cut 1).
Cut out pattern pieces as directed. 1 cm seams and edges and 2 cm hem allowed. Join all pieces together with right sides facing. Exposed raw edges can be neatened by overlocking, zigzagging, or simply left raw, as knit fabric will not fray.

TO MAKE

1 Decide which motifs from your contrast print you want to applique (we used two). Carefully cut out, allowing 6 mm allowance from your intended stitching line. Place motifs carefully on to front to form desired design. Pin securely.
2 Using a small machine stitch, sew motifs around stitching line. Trim fabric away very close to stitching. Using narrow, closely-spaced zigzag, stitch over first stitching line to cover raw edge. Press. We suggest you practise a test applique first with some spare fabric.
3 Stitch shoulder seams. Press. Stitch side seams. Press.
4 Turn under 1 cm at neck edge. Press. Topstitch and edgestitch to finish. Repeat for armholes.
5 Turn hem up to suit. Trim to 2 cm. Topstitch and edgestitch hem to finish.

SHORT TUBE SKIRT

SIZE: Age 12 years

MATERIALS

- **60 cm of 150 cm wide cotton knit fabric**
- **60 cm of 2 cm wide elastic**

PATTERN

Cut two rectangles for skirt, 46 cm wide x 60 cm long. 1 cm seams and hem allowed. 5 cm turning allowed at waist. Join together with right sides facing. Exposed raw edges can be neatened by overlocking, zigzagging, or simply left raw, as knit fabric will not fray.

TO MAKE

1 Stitch side seams from waist to a point 24 cm above hem, to allow for slits. Press open.
2 To form waist frill and casing for elastic, turn under 5 cm at waist edge. Press. Stitch around waist 2 cm from edge. Stitch again around waist 2.5 cm below first row of stitching, leaving gap at centre back for inserting elastic. Cut elastic to fit waist, insert and join ends. Stitch gap closed.
3 Measure hem to suit, keeping 1 cm allowance. Cut lower corners of slits to a gentle curve. Press under 1 cm around slits and hem. Topstitch and edge-stitch around slits and hem to finish.

PANELLED SWIMSUIT

SIZE: Age 12 years

MATERIALS

- **yellow, 40 cm long x 40 cm wide Lycra (2-way stretch fabric)**
- **red, 40 cm long x 40 cm wide Lycra**
- **green, 40 cm long x 40 cm wide Lycra**
- **2.50 m of 1 cm wide swimwear elastic**

PATTERN

See Pattern 18

Right Front (cut 1 red), Left Front (cut 1 yellow), Lower Front (cut 1 green), Right Back (cut 1 red), Left Back (cut 1 yellow), Lower Back (cut 2 green), Gusset (cut 1 green).
Cut out pattern pieces as directed. 1 cm seams and edges allowed. Join all pieces together with right sides facing. Exposed raw edges can be neatened by overlocking, zigzagging, or simply left raw, as knit fabric will not fray.

TO MAKE

1 Stitch left front to left of lower front from side to centre front point. Stitch right front to left from neck to side, matching centre front points.
2 Stitch left back to left lower back from side to centre back. Repeat for right pieces. Stitch centre back seam from neck to crotch.
3 Placing gusset on top of back, stitch crotch seam through resulting three layers. Covering seam, pull gusset to front. Stitch to front at leg edges. Stitch side seams and shoulder seams.
4 Cut elastic to fit snugly around neck edge. Join ends. Mark neck edge and elastic into quarters. Pin elastic evenly around inside neck edge matching markings. Stitch with zigzag so elasticised edge will stretch. Turn edge under 1 cm. Zigzag stitch to finish. Repeat for armhole and leg edges.

Girl's singlet top and short tube skirt (instructions page 32)

SPORT SHORTS

SIZE: M/L Man

MATERIALS
- [ ] **80 cm of 150 cm wide cotton interlock fabric**
- [ ] **80 cm of 2 cm wide elastic**

PATTERN
See Pattern 16 (short length)
Front (cut 2), Back (cut 2), Pocket (cut 4).
Cut out pattern pieces as directed. 1 cm seams and 2 cm hems allowed. Join all pieces together with right sides facing. Exposed raw edges can be neatened by overlocking, zigzagging, or simply left raw, as knit fabric will not fray.

TO MAKE
1 Stitch long straight edge of pockets to side seams, matching notches. Press.
2 Just inside pocket seam, stitch side seams of pants from waist down to upper notch. Just inside pocket seam, stitch side seams from lower notch down to a point 4 cm above hem. Press seam open. Stitch curved edges of pockets together.
3 Stitch inside leg seams. Press. Stitch around crotch seam from front waist to back waist, matching inside leg seam points. Press.
4 To form casing for elastic, turn under 3 cm at waist edge. Press. Stitch around waist 2.5 cm from edge, leaving gap at centre back for inserting elastic. Cut elastic to fit waist, insert and join ends. Stitch gap closed.
5 Turn hem up 2 cm, with short slit at side seam. Press. Topstitch and edgestitch to finish.

SQUARE NECK RAGLAN TOP

SIZE: M/L Man

MATERIALS
- [ ] **1.20 cm of 150 cm wide cotton knit fabric**

PATTERN
See Pattern 19 (low neck, short sleeve)
Front (cut 1), Back (cut 1), Sleeve (cut 2).
Cut out pattern pieces as directed. 1 cm seams and 2 cm hems and edges allowed. Join all pieces together with right sides facing. Exposed raw edges can be neatened by overlocking, zigzagging, or simply left raw, as knit fabric will not fray.

TO MAKE
1 Turn under 2 cm at neck edges of front, back, and sleeves. Press. Topstitch and edgestitch to finish.
2 Stitch sleeves to front and back along armhole seams, very carefully matching neck edges. Press.
3 Stitch front to back along underarm seams, matching underarm points. Press.
4 Turn sleeve hems up to suit. Trim to 2 cm. Topstitch and edgestitch to finish. Repeat for hem.

RAGLAN ZIP-UP JACKET

SIZE: M/L Man

MATERIALS
- [ ] **1.80 m of 150 cm wide cotton interlock fabric**
- [ ] **65 cm open-ended nylon zipper**
- [ ] **2.70 m of 1.5 cm wide elastic**

PATTERN
See Pattern 19 (high neck, long sleeve)
Front (cut 1), Back (cut 1), Sleeve (cut 2), Pocket (cut 2), Collar (cut 1).
Cut out pattern pieces as directed. 1 cm seams allowed except where specified. Join all pieces together with right sides facing. Exposed raw edges can be neatened by overlocking, zigzagging, or simply left raw, as knit fabric will not fray.

TO MAKE
1 Fold under 3 cm at top edge of pocket. Press. Topstitch and edgestitch. Fold under 1 cm at front edge of pocket. Press. Pin pocket on jacket front so that raw edges at side seam and hem match. Topstitch and edgestitch pocket front to jacket. Repeat for other pocket.
2 Stitch sleeves to body around armholes, matching notches. Press. Stitch front to back along underarm seams, matching underarm points, and catching pockets into side seams as you go. Press.
3 To form elasticised hem, turn under 5 cm at hem edge. Press. Stitch around hem 2 cm from edge, and again 4 cm from edge. Cut elastic to fit comfortably. Insert elastic through openings at centre front, and stitch ends to centre front.
4 To form elasticised cuff, turn under 5 cm at sleeve end. Press. Stitch around hem 2 cm from edge, and again 4 cm from edge, leaving gaps for inserting elastic at underarm seam. Cut elastic to fit comfortably. Insert elastic and stitch ends.

Stitch gaps closed. Repeat for other cuff.
5 Press in 1.5 cm seam allowances on centre front opening. Sew zipper into place beneath pressed edges with lower end level with jacket hem, and upper end just below neck seam allowance.
6 Fold collar in half along length, right sides facing. Stitch ends. Trim and turn to right side. Pin undercollar evenly around neck edge, matching notches. Stitch. Trim seams and clip where needed. Press seams to inside collar. Press under 1 cm at uppercollar edge, and pin in place over neck seam, enclosing all raw edges. Slip-stitch or machine stitch opening to close. Topstitch and edgestitch around collar edge to finish.

SQUARE NECK RAGLAN TOP

SIZE: 12/14

MATERIALS
- [ ] **1 m of 150 cm wide cotton knit fabric**

PATTERN and TO MAKE
As for SQUARE NECK RAGLAN TOP on this page.

DRAWSTRING SHORTS

SIZE: 10/12/14

MATERIALS
- ☐ **80 cm of 150 cm wide cotton knit fabric**
- ☐ **70 cm of 2 cm wide elastic**
- ☐ **80 cm of cotton rope for fake drawstring**

PATTERN
See Pattern 8 (short length)
Front (cut 2), Back (cut 2), Pocket (cut 4). Waist Casing, cut strip 110 cm x 8 cm.
Cut out pattern pieces as directed. 1 cm seams and 2 cm hems allowed. Join all pieces together with right sides facing. Exposed raw edges can be neatened by overlocking, zigzagging, or simply left raw, as knit fabric will not fray.

TO MAKE
1   Stitch long straight edge of pockets to side seams, matching notches. Press.
2   Just inside pocket seam, stitch side seams of pants from waist down to upper notch. Just inside pocket seam, stitch side seams from lower notch down to hem. Press. Stitch curved edges of pockets together.
3   Stitch inside leg seams. Press. Stitch around crotch seam from front waist to back waist, matching inside leg seam points. Press.
4   Stitch short ends of waist casing strip. Press. Fold casing in half along length with seams inside. With seam at centre back, pin casing to shorts evenly around waist. Stitch, leaving gap at centre back for inserting elastic. Cut elastic to fit waist, insert and join ends. Stitch gap closed. Stitch rope at centre front, knot ends and tie bow.
5   Turn hem up to suit. Press. Trim to 2 cm. Topstitch and edgestitch to finish.

SHORT TUBE SKIRT

SIZE: Age 12 years

MATERIALS
- ☐ **60 cm of 150 cm wide cotton knit fabric**
- ☐ **60 cm of 2 cm wide elastic**

PATTERN
Cut rectangle for skirt, 96 cm wide x 56 cm long. 2 cm centre back seam and hem allowed. 3 cm turning allowed at waist. Join together with right sides facing. Exposed raw edges can be neatened by overlocking, zigzagging, or simply left raw, as knit fabric will not fray.

TO MAKE
1   Stitch centre back seam from waist to a point 22 cm above hem, to allow for slit. Press open, and continue pressing under 2 cm at slit.
2   Turn hem up to suit. Press. Trim to 2 cm. Mitre corners of slit at hem, trim and press. Topstitch and edgestitch down centre back slit and around hem to finish.
3   To form casing for elastic, turn under 3 cm at waist edge. Press. Stitch around waist 2.5 cm from edge, leaving gap at centre back for inserting elastic. Cut elastic to fit waist, insert and join ends. Stitch gap closed.

SINGLET TOP

SIZE: Age 12 years

MATERIALS
- ☐ **60 cm of 150 cm wide cotton knit fabric**

PATTERN
See Pattern 20
Front (cut 1), Back (cut 1).
Cut out pattern pieces as directed. 1 cm seams and edges, and 2 cm hem allowed. Join all pieces together with right sides facing. Exposed raw edges can be neatened by overlocking, zigzagging, or simply left raw, as knit fabric will not fray.

TO MAKE
1   Stitch side and shoulder seams. Press.
2   Turn under 1 cm at neck edge. Press. Topstitch and edgestitch to finish. Repeat process for armholes.
3   Turn under 2 cm allowance at hem. Press. Topstitch and edgestitch to finish.

Swimsuit and sarong skirt (instructions page 34)

The pattern for these warm and cosy tracksuits doubles for winter ski-pyjamas. Make them for all the family in no time at all!

Woman's sweatshirt and track pants (instructions page 35)

PATTERN

See Pattern 16 (long length)
Front Leg (cut 2), Back Leg (cut 2), Pocket (cut 4). Ribbing Ankle Cuffs, cut two 14 cm long x 28 cm wide.

Cut out pattern pieces as directed. 1 cm seams allowed. Join all pieces together with right sides facing. Exposed raw edges can be neatened by overlocking, zigzagging, or simply left raw, as knit fabric will not fray.

TO MAKE

1 Stitch long straight edge of pockets to side seams, matching notches. Press.
2 Just inside pocket seam, stitch side seams of pants from waist down to upper notch. Just inside pocket seam, stitch side seams from lower notch down to hem. Press. Stitch curved edges of pockets together.
3 Stitch inside leg seams. Press. Stitch around crotch seam from front waist to back waist, matching inside leg seam points. Press.
4 To form casing for elastic, turn under 3 cm at waist edge. Press. Stitch around waist 2.5 cm from edge, leaving gap at centre back for inserting elastic. Cut elastic to fit waist, insert and join ends. Stitch gap closed.
5 Stitch short edges of ankle ribbing to form tube. Fold in half with seams inside. Pin evenly around leg ends with raw edges and seams matching. Stitch with overlocking or zigzagging so that opening will stretch sufficiently. Press seam away from ribbing.

SWEATSHIRT

SIZE: M/L Man

MATERIALS
- ☐ **1. 30 m of 160 cm wide fleecy knit fabric**
- ☐ **20 cm long of 120 cm wide contrast fleecy knit fabric for sleeve bands**
- ☐ **40 cm of 90 cm wide ribbing**
- ☐ **50 cm narrow stay-tape for shoulder seams**

PATTERN
See Pattern 15 (long sleeve)
Cut ribbing as follows:
Neck, 8 cm long x 38 cm wide. Hipband, 14 cm long x 90 cm wide. Cuffs, two 14 cm long x 28 cm wide.
Front (cut 1), Back (cut 1), Sleeve (cut 2). Stitching lines for contrast band are marked on pattern. Add 1 cm seam allowances on main sleeve pieces **and** contrast bands before cutting.

Cut out pattern pieces as directed. 1 cm seams allowed. Join all pieces together with right sides facing. Exposed raw edges can be neatened by overlocking, zigzagging, or simply left raw, as knit fabric will not fray.

TO MAKE
First stitch contrast bands to main sleeve pieces, matching side seam points, to form complete sleeves. Press.
Continue to make as for SWEATSHIRT on page 10.

TRACK PANTS

SIZE: M/L Man

MATERIALS
- ☐ **1. 70 m of 160 cm wide red fleecy knit fabric**
- ☐ **20 cm of 80 cm wide ribbing**
- ☐ **80 cm of 2 cm wide elastic**

Join ends. Mark waist edge and elastic into quarters. Pin elastic evenly around inside waist edge matching markings. Stitch with zigzag so elasticised edge will stretch. Turn edge under 1 cm. Zigzag stitch to finish. Repeat for leg edges.

T-SHIRT

SIZE: Age 6 years

MATERIALS
- [ ] **50 cm of 150 cm wide cotton knit fabric**
- [ ] **10 cm of 40 cm wide ribbing**
- [ ] **30 cm narrow stay-tape for shoulder seams**

PATTERN
See Pattern 9
Front (cut 1), Back (cut 1), Sleeve (cut 2). Cut out pattern pieces as directed. Neck band ribbing, cut 6 cm long x 32 cm wide. 1 cm seams and 2 cm hems allowed. Join all pieces together with right sides facing. Exposed raw edges can be neatened by overlocking, zigzagging, or simply left raw, as knit fabric will not fray.

TO MAKE
1 Stitch shoulder seams, attaching stay-tape as you sew. Press. Stitch sleeves to body around armholes, matching notches. Press. Stitch front to back along underarm seams, matching underarm points. Press.
2 Stitch short edges of neck ribbing to form tube. Fold in half with seams inside. Pin evenly around neck with raw edges matching, and ribbing seam at centre back. Stitch with overlocking or zigzagging so that neck opening will stretch sufficiently. Press seam away from ribbing.
7 Turn under 2 cm at sleeve hem. Press. Topstitch and edgestitch to finish. Turn hem up to suit. Press. Trim to 2 cm. Topstitch and edgestitch to finish.

SWIM TRUNKS

SIZE: Age 6 years

MATERIALS
- [ ] **60 cm long x 30 cm wide Lycra (2-way stretch fabric)**
- [ ] **scraps of contrast colour Lycra for side panels**
- [ ] **scrap of contrast print knit fabric for applique**
- [ ] **1 m of 1 cm wide swimwear elastic**

PATTERN
See Pattern 21
Front and Back (cut 1), Side Panel (cut 2). Cut out pattern pieces as directed. 1 cm seams and edges allowed. Join together with right sides facing. Exposed raw edges can be neatened by overlocking, zigzagging, or simply left raw, as knit fabric will not fray.

TO MAKE
1 Decide which motif from your contrast print you want to applique. Carefully cut out, allowing 6 mm allowance from your intended stitching line. Place motif carefully on to left front in desired position. Pin securely.
2 Using a small machine stitch, sew motif around stitching line. Trim fabric away very close to stitching. Using narrow, closely-spaced zigzag, stitch over first stitching line to cover raw edge. Press. We suggest you practise a test applique first with some spare fabris.
3 Stitch side seams.
4 Cut elastic to fit snugly around waist.

STITCHED SWIMSUIT

SIZE: 10

MATERIALS
- [ ] **80 cm of 90 cm wide Lycra (2-way stretch fabric)**
- [ ] **3.30 m of 1 cm wide swimwear elastic**

PATTERN
See Pattern 22
Front (cut 1), Back (cut 1), Gusset (cut 1). Cut out pattern pieces as directed. 1 cm seams and edges allowed. Join all pieces together with right sides facing. Exposed raw edges can be neatened by overlocking, zigzagging, or simply left raw, as knit fabric will not fray.

TO MAKE
1 With removable chalk lines, copy stitching lines from pattern on to right side of front and back. Fold along chalk lines and pin curved 'tucks' in place. Using a narrow zigzag, stitch just inside folded edge.
2 Placing gusset on top of back, stitch crotch seam through resulting three layers. Covering seam, pull gusset to front. Stitch to front at leg edges. Stitch side seams and shoulder seams.
3 Cut elastic to fit snugly around neck edge. Join ends. Mark neck edge and elastic into quarters. Pin elastic evenly around inside neck edge matching markings. Stitch with zigzag so elasticised edge will stretch. Turn edge under 1 cm. Zigzag stitch to finish. Repeat for armhole and leg edges.

SARONG SKIRT

SIZE: 10/12/14

MATERIALS
- [ ] **1.5 m of 150 cm wide cotton knit fabric**
- [ ] **80 cm narrow stay-tape for waist**

PATTERN
See Pattern 23
Skirt (cut 1), Tie (cut 4).
Cut out pattern pieces as directed. 1 cm seams and 2 cm hem allowed. Join all

pieces together with right sides facing. Exposed raw edges can be neatened by overlocking, zigzagging, or simply left raw, as knit fabric will not fray.

TO MAKE

1   Cut stay-tape to fit low waist. Stitch to waist raw edge. Turn under 1 cm at waist. Press. Turn under 1 cm again. Press. Topstitch and edgestitch to finish.

2   Pin pleats in skirt as marked on pattern. Stitch just inside 1 cm seam allowance to secure.

3   With right sides together, stitch one pair of ties around long sides and diagonal end. Trim seams and corners and turn to right side. Press. Repeat instruction for other tie.

4   Carefully stitching right up to each end, and with right sides together, stitch front of one tie to skirt side from waist to bottom of pleats, and covering original stitches. Long edge of tie should be at the top. Clip skirt raw edge almost to stitching line at bottom of tie so that seam can be pressed towards tie. Turn under raw edge on back of tie. Press. Slipstitch to close. Topstitch and edgestitch right around tie. Repeat all steps for other tie.

5   Stitch side seam from hem up to notch at bottom of small gap. Press, and continue pressing under 1 cm on gap. Edgestitch gap to finish.

6   Turn hem up to suit. Press. Trim to 2 cm. Topstitch and edgestitch to finish.

SINGLET DRESS

SIZE: Age 12 years

MATERIALS
☐ **50 cm of 150 cm wide cotton knit fabric**
☐ **60 cm of 80 cm wide ribbing**

PATTERN
See Pattern 20
Front (cut 1), Back (cut 1) from ribbing. Cut ribbing in two widths of 40 cm and stretch slightly to fit pattern as you pin each pattern piece for cutting.
From cotton knit fabric, cut skirt 36 cm long x 150 cm wide. Cut two 5 cm strips across width of fabric to give you 60 cm strip for neck binding and two 48 cm strips for armhole bindings.
1 cm seams and 2 cm hem allowed. Join all pieces together with right sides facing. Exposed raw edges can be neatened by overlocking, zigzagging, or simply left raw, as knit fabric will not fray.

TO MAKE

1   Stitch shoulder seams. Press.

2   Stitch short ends of neck binding. Press. Fold in half along length and press. With join at centre back, pin binding evenly around neck with raw edges even and right sides facing. Stitch. Press seam away from binding.

3   Stitch side seams. Press. Make armhole bindings in the same manner as neck binding, placing joins at underarms.

4   Mark top and skirt waist edges in quarters. Pin together evenly around waist matching markings and with skirt seam matching left side seam. Stitch. Press.

5   Turn hem up to suit. Press. Trim allowance to 2 cm. Topstitch and edgestitch hem to finish.

SWEATSHIRT

SIZE: 12/14

MATERIALS
☐ **1. 30 m of 140 cm wide cotton knit fabric**
☐ **30 cm of 90 cm wide ribbing**
☐ **50 cm narrow stay-tape for shoulder seams**

PATTERN
See Pattern 1 (long sleeve)
Cut ribbing as follows:
Neck, 8 cm long x 36 cm wide. Hipband, 14 cm long x 84 cm wide. Cuffs, two 14 cm long x 20 cm wide.

Front (cut 1), Back (cut 1), Sleeve (cut 2). Cut out pattern pieces as directed. 1 cm seams allowed. Join all pieces together with right sides facing. Exposed raw edges can be neatened by overlocking, zigzagging, or simply left raw, as knit fabric will not fray.

TO MAKE
As for SWEATSHIRT on page 10.

TRACK PANTS

SIZE: 10/12/14

MATERIALS
☐ **1. 40 m of 150 cm wide cotton knit fabric**
☐ **20 cm of 60 cm wide ribbing**
☐ **70 cm of 2 cm wide elastic**

PATTERN
See Pattern 8 (long length)
Front Leg (cut 2), Back Leg (cut 2), Pocket (cut 4). Ribbing Ankle Cuffs, cut two 14 cm long x 28 cm wide.
Cut out pattern pieces as directed. 1 cm seams allowed. Join all pieces together with right sides facing. Exposed raw edges can be neatened by overlocking, zigzagging, or simply left raw, as knit fabric will not fray.

TO MAKE
As for TRACK PANTS on page 33.

Holiday Fun

Relaxed and casual get away – a no-rush 'time-table' of pool, tennis court, beach, spa, dinner on the terrace – that's what today's resorts and holiday spots offer us. We help you look the part with our patterns for a sarong skirt, swimsuit and sexy separates in a collection of pieces that go together beautifully.

Since just a few stretch fabric garments will take you from poolside through to dancing at night, your luggage will be as light and easy as the gentle breezes on the terrace! For even more go-together ideas, look at the patterns in our Beach Sports chapter.

Oh, and don't forget to write!

CHOOSE THE COLOURS THAT SUIT YOU!

We're all guilty of choosing the same old colours, but what many of us ignore is the fact that we all have a group of colours that are just perfect for our own particular colouring. The trick is to discover this group and stick to it! Almost all of us can wear most colours, but it is the shade of the colour that matters most.

When you know your grouping, you will automatically eliminate colours that are unflattering, and head for those that will bring you compliments.

We can group these colour families as you would for the seasons of the year.

SUMMER
Summer colours are pastel, soft and cool, with blue undertones. They are not vivid or brassy. Light brown or true blonde hair often suits Summer colours.

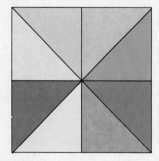

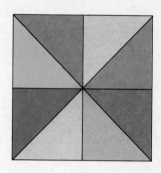

AUTUMN
Autumn colours have strong orange and brown undertones and usually suit red-headed people.

WINTER
Winter colours have stronger blue undertones than Summer colours, and contain the basics, black and white. These colours are vivid or even icy. Sallow complexions usually suit Winter colours.

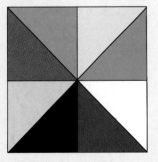

SPRING
Spring colours have clear yellow undertones. They are delicate rather than vivid.

The best way to choose your group is to select several shades of one colour, hold them against your face, and then it's over to the mirror! You will soon see which group emerges as your special selection.

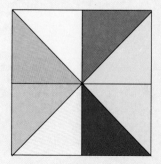

CIRCULAR SKIRT

SIZE: 10/12

MATERIALS
- [ ] **3.80 m of 150 cm wide cotton knit fabric**
- [ ] **70 cm of 10 cm wide frilled edge waist elastic**

PATTERN
See Pattern 2 (pocket only) page 71
Draw quarter-circle for skirt pattern as follows:
1 Draw square on paper 110 cm x 110 cm.
2 From the point of one corner, with a radius of 15 cm, draw a small quarter-circle (for quarter-waist seam of 24 cm).
3 From the same point, with a radius of 110 cm, draw a large quarter-circle for skirt hem.
4 Mark one straight edge with 'centre front/centre back, place on fold', and the other straight edge with 'side seam, place along straight grain of fabric'. Label pattern piece with 'front/back circular skirt. Cut 1 front and 1 back, both on fold'.
5 Mark notches for pocket opening on side seam, 4 cm and 20 cm down from waist.

Front Skirt (cut 1), Back Skirt (cut 1), Pocket (cut 4).
Cut out pattern pieces as directed. 1 cm seams and 2 cm hem allowed. Join all pieces together with right sides facing. Exposed raw edges can be neatened by overlocking, zigzagging, or simply left raw, as knit fabric will not fray.

TO MAKE
1 Stitch long straight edge of pockets to side seams, matching notches. Press.
2 Just inside pocket seam, stitch side seams of skirt from waist down to upper notch. Just inside pocket seam, stitch side seams from lower notch down to hem. Stitch curved edges of pockets together. Press.
3 Stitch elastic ends to fit waist, forming waistband. Topstitch. Mark lower edge of waistband and skirt waist into quarters. Pin waistband on top of skirt evenly around waist matching markings. Stitch together along top of small elastic frill.
4 Allow skirt to hang for a week before levelling hem to suit, allowing a 2 cm hem. Preferably, level the hem while it is being worn. Press under, topstitch and edge-stitch to finish.

GYPSY TOP

SIZE: 10/12/14

MATERIALS
- ☐ **1.10 m of 180 cm wide cotton single knit fabric**
- ☐ **150 cm of 1 cm wide elastic**

PATTERN
See Pattern 24

Front (cut 1), Back (cut 1), Sleeve (cut 2). Cut one length of elastic of 90 cm for neck and two lengths of 30 cm each for sleeves. Cut out pattern pieces as directed. 1 cm seams and 2 cm hems and edges allowed. Join all pieces together with right sides facing. Exposed raw edges can be neatened by overlocking, zigzagging, or simply left raw, as knit fabric will not fray.

TO MAKE
1   Stitch sleeves to front and back, matching notches. Press. Stitch front to back along underarm seam, matching underarm points. Press.

2   To form casing for elastic, turn under 2 cm at neck edge. Press. Stitch around neck 1.5 cm from edge, leaving gap at centre back for inserting elastic. Insert elastic and join ends. Stitch gap closed. Repeat for lower edge of sleeves.

3   Turn under 2 cm at hem. Press. Topstitch and edgestitch to finish.

WRAP-AROUND TOP

SIZE: 10/12/14

MATERIALS, PATTERN and TO MAKE

As for WRAP-AROUND TOP on page 16.

TUBE SKIRTS

SIZE: 10/12
Measurements for short skirt in brackets

MATERIALS

- ☐ **1 m (60 cm) of 150 cm wide cotton knit fabric**
- ☐ **70 cm of 2 cm wide elastic**

PATTERN

Cut rectangle for skirt, 102 cm wide x 98 cm (55 cm) long. 2 cm centre back seam and hem allowed. 3 cm turning allowed at waist. Join together with right sides facing. Exposed raw edges can be neatened by overlocking, zigzagging, or simply left raw, as knit fabric will not fray.

TO MAKE

1 Stitch centre back seam from waist to a point 34 cm (22 cm) above hem, to allow for slit. Press open, and continue pressing under 2 cm at slit. (You may prefer to omit the slit on the short skirt.)

2 Turn hem up to suit. Press. Trim to 2 cm. Mitre corners of slit at hem, trim and press. Topstitch and edgestitch down centre back slit and around hem to finish.

3 To form casing for elastic, turn under 3 cm at waist edge. Press. Edgestitch at fold, and again around waist 2.5 cm from edge, leaving gap at centre back for inserting elastic. Cut elastic to fit waist, insert and join ends. Stitch gap closed.

Two very different looks – using the same patterns!

SINGLET TOP WITH APPLIQUE

SIZE: Age 12 years

MATERIALS
- [ ] **60 cm of 150 cm wide cotton knit fabric**
- [ ] **scraps of contrast print cotton knit fabric for applique**

PATTERN
See Pattern 20
Front (cut 1), Back (cut 1).
Cut out pattern pieces as directed. 1 cm seams and edges, and 2 cm hem allowed. Join all pieces together with right sides facing. Exposed raw edges can be neatened by overlocking, zigzagging, or simply left raw, as knit fabric will not fray.

TO MAKE
1   Decide which motifs from your contrast print you want to applique (we used six different motifs). Carefully cut them out, allowing 6 mm allowance from your intended stitching line. Place motifs carefully onto singlet front to form desired design, keeping well inside turning allowed for neck and armhole. Pin securely.
2   Using a small machine stitch, sew each motif to singlet around stitching line. Trim fabric away very close to stitching. Using narrow, closely-spaced zigzag, stitch over first stitching line to cover raw edge. Press. We suggest you practise a test applique first with some spare fabric.
3   Stitch side and shoulder seams. Press.
4   Turn under 1 cm at neck edge. Press. Topstitch and edgestitch to finish. Repeat process for armholes.
5   Turn under 2 cm at hem. Press. Topstitch and edgestitch to finish.

CIRCULAR SKIRT

SIZE: Age 12 years

MATERIALS
- [ ] **3 m of 150 cm wide cotton knit fabric**
- [ ] **60 cm of 10 cm wide frilled-edge waist elastic**

PATTERN
See Pattern 2 (pocket only) page 71
Draw quarter-circle for skirt pattern as follows:
1   Draw square on paper 90 cm x 90 cm.
2   From the point of one corner, with a radius of 13 cm, draw a small quarter-circle (for quarter-waist seam of 21 cm).
3   From the same point, with a radius of 90 cm, draw a large quarter-circle for skirt hem.
4   Mark one straight edge with 'centre front/centre back, place on fold', and the other straight edge with 'side seam, place along straight grain of fabric'. Label pattern piece with 'front/back circular skirt. Cut 1 front and 1 back, both on fold'.
5   Mark notches for pocket opening on side seam, 4 cm and 20 cm down from waist.

Front Skirt (cut 1), Back Skirt (cut 1), Pocket (cut 4).
Cut out pattern pieces as directed. 1 cm seams and 2 cm hem allowed. Join all pieces together with right sides facing. Exposed raw edges can be neatened by overlocking, zigzagging, or simply left raw, as knit fabric will not fray.

TO MAKE
As for CIRCULAR SKIRT on page 38.

SINGLET TOP

SIZE: 10/12

MATERIALS
- ☐ **70 cm of 150 cm wide cotton knit fabric**
- ☐ **8 cm strip of 150 cm wide contrast cotton knit fabric for bindings**

PATTERN
See Pattern 25 (short length)
Front (cut 1), Back (cut 1).
Cut out pattern pieces as directed. Cut two 4 cm strips across width of contrast fabric to give you 86 cm for neck binding and two 54 cm for armhole bindings. 1 cm seams and 2 cm hem allowed. Join all pieces together with right sides facing. Exposed raw edges can be neatened by overlocking, zigzagging, or simply left raw, as knit fabric will not fray.

TO MAKE
1 Stitch shoulder seams. Press.
2 Stitch short ends of neck binding. Press. With join at centre back, pin binding evenly around neck with raw edges even and right sides facing. Stitch. Turn half width of binding to inside. Press. On the outside, stitch around neck in gutter of binding seam to secure inside of binding.
3 Stitch side seams. Press. Make armhole bindings in the same manner as neck binding, placing joins at underarms.
4 Turn hem up to suit. Press. Trim allowance to 2 cm. Topstitch and edgestitch hem to finish.

EIGHT GORE SKIRT

SIZE: 10/12

MATERIALS, PATTERN and TO MAKE
As for EIGHT GORE SKIRT on page 15.

SHORT SINGLET TOP

SIZE: 10/12

MATERIALS
- ☐ **40 cm of 150 cm wide cotton knit fabric**
- ☐ **30 cm x 30 cm of contrast cotton knit fabric for centre front panel**

PATTERN
See Pattern 26

HINT

If using a commercial pattern that states 'for stretch fabrics only' do not vary from this rule and use a woven fabric! Stretch patterns are cut taking into account the amount of stretch the fabric has – as this will affect the garment's fit. You may end up with a garment that is much smaller than you intended, without this 'built-in' stretch.

You can, on the other hand, use knit fabrics for almost any pattern designed to be used with conventional fabrics.

Centre Front (cut 1), Side Back (cut 1). Cut out pattern pieces as directed. 1.5 cm seams and hems allowed. Join pieces together with right sides facing. Exposed raw edges can be neatened by overlocking, zigzagging, or simply left raw, as knit fabric will not fray.

TO MAKE

1 Turn under 1.5 cm on slightly curved top edge of centre front piece. Press. Topstitch and edgestitch.

2 Stitch shoulder seams. Press. Stitch sides of centre front to sides of side back from bottom edge, matching top edge of centre front to notch. Press seam towards side back, and continue pressing around neck turning under 1.5 cm allowance on edge.

3 Topstitch and edgestitch on one side from lower edge up to and around neck and down to lower edge on other side, catching seams down and forming neck finish as you go.

4 Turn under 1.5 cm at armhole. Press. Topstitch and edgestitch. Repeat for hem.

SARONG SKIRT

SIZE: 10/12/14

MATERIALS

☐ **1.5 m of 150 cm wide cotton knit fabric**

☐ **80 cm narrow stay-tape for waist**

PATTERN

See Pattern 23
Skirt (cut 1), Tie (cut 4).
Cut out pattern pieces as directed. 1 cm seams and 2 cm hem allowed. Join all pieces together with right sides facing. Exposed raw edges can be neatened by overlocking, zigzagging, or simply left raw, as knit fabric will not fray.

TO MAKE

1 Cut stay-tape to fit low waist. Stitch to waist raw edge. Turn under 1 cm at waist. Press. Turn under 1 cm again. Press. Topstitch and edgestitch to finish.

2 Pin pleats in skirt as marked on pattern. Stitch just inside 1 cm seam allowance to secure.

3 With right sides together, stitch one pair of ties around long sides and diagonal end. Trim seams and corners and turn to right side. Press. Repeat instruction for other tie.

4 Carefully stitching right up to each end, and with right sides together, stitch front of one tie to skirt side from waist to bottom of pleats, and covering original stitches. Long edge of tie should be at the top. Clip skirt raw edge almost to stitching line at bottom of tie so that seam can be pressed towards tie. Turn under raw edge on back of tie. Press. Slipstitch to close. Topstitch and edgestitch right around tie. Repeat all steps for other tie.

5 Stitch side seam from hem up to notch at bottom of small gap. Press, and continue pressing under 1 cm on gap. Edgestitch gap to finish.

6 Turn hem up to suit. Press. Trim to 2 cm. Topstitch and edgestitch to finish.

HINT

Edgestitching and topstitching for a trim effect will be straight if you use the edge of your presser foot as your guide. As you stitch, carefully keep the foot edge aligned with the fabric edge, and your rows of stitching will always be straight.

Ready for Bed

You'll have sweet dreams every night in this great sleepwear – there are no buttons to prod you or stiff fabric to constrict you and there is a style to suit every member of your family!

The patterns range from a sleepsuit with feet, for the smallest and (we hope) the sleepiest member of the family, through to comfy pyjamas that even the largest man will love.

And the patterns are so versatile! A singlet or T shirt can become a short or long nightdress or even a cover up for the beach, while the family tracksuit patterns will make the cosiest winter pyjamas.

If you agree that this sleepwear looks too good to be always hidden away under the blankets, remember that they are just perfect for a little weekend lounging – reading the papers, having a late breakfast and not even thinking of getting dressed until around midday.

We won't tell a soul!

T-SHIRT NIGHTIE

SIZE: 12/14

MATERIALS

- ☐ **1.20 m of 150 cm wide cotton knit fabric**
- ☐ **10 cm of 70 cm wide ribbing**
- ☐ **50 cm narrow stay-tape for shoulder seams**

PATTERN

See Pattern 1 (V-neck, short sleeve, long length)
Front (cut 1), Back (cut 1), Sleeve, (cut 2). Neck Ribbing (cut 1 from Pattern 15).
Cut out pattern pieces as directed. 1 cm seams and 2 cm hems allowed. Join all pieces together with right sides facing. Exposed raw edges can be neatened by overlocking, zigzagging, or simply left raw, as knit fabric will not fray.

TO MAKE

1   Stitch shoulder seams, attaching stay-tape as you sew. Press.
2   Fold neck ribbing in half along length. Lay ends one on top of the other, in a neat V and matching raw edges. Pin evenly around neck with centre front points and raw edges matching. Stitch, snipping nightie centre front point almost to stitching so you can stitch around the V. Press seam away from ribbing.
3   Stitch sleeves to body around armholes, matching notches. Press. Stitch front to back along underarm seams, matching underarm points. Press.
4   Turn under 2 cm at sleeve hem. Press. Topstitch and edgestitch to finish. Turn curved hem up to suit. Press. Trim to 2 cm. Topstitch and edgestitch to finish.

SINGLET NIGHTIE

SIZE: 10/12

MATERIALS

- ☐ **1 m of 150 cm wide cotton knit fabric**
- ☐ **20 cm of 80 cm wide ribbing**

PATTERN

See Pattern 25 (long length, low neck)
Front (cut 1), Back (cut 1).
Cut out pattern pieces as directed. Cut ribbing in three 4 cm strips across width to give you one 90 cm strip for neck binding, two 54 cm strips for armhole bindings, and two 65 cm strips for hem binding.

1 cm seams allowed. Join all pieces together with right sides facing. Exposed raw edges can be neatened by overlocking, zigzagging, or simply left raw, as knit fabric will not fray.

TO MAKE

1   Stitch shoulder seams. Press.
2   Stitch short ends of neck binding. Press. Fold in half along length. With join at centre back, pin binding evenly around neck with raw edges even and right sides facing. Stitch. Press seam away from binding. Edgestitch to finish.
3   Stitch side seams. Press. Make armhole bindings in the same manner as neck binding, placing joins at underarms.
4   Make hem bindings in the same manner, placing joins at side seams.

HOODED ROBE

SIZE: 10/12

MATERIALS

- ☐ **3.20 m of 150 cm wide stretch towelling fabric**
- ☐ **70 cm narrow stay-tape for shoulder seam and back neck**

PATTERN

See Pattern 28
Front (cut 2), Back (cut 1), Sleeve, (cut 2). Hood and Front Yoke (cut 2), Pocket (cut 2), Belt (cut 2).
Cut out pattern pieces as directed. Cut strip 40 cm long x 4 cm wide for two belt loops. 1 cm seams and 2 cm hems allowed. Join all pieces together with right sides facing. Exposed raw edges can be neatened by overlocking, zigzagging, or simply left raw, as knit fabric will not fray.

TO MAKE

1   Turn under 4 cm at top edge of pocket. Press. Topstitch. Press under 1 cm at front and lower edges of pocket. Place pocket on robe front where comfortable, with raw edges at side seam matching. Pin then edgestitch pocket to robe. Repeat for other pocket.
2   To make belt loops, fold long edges of strip to centre, then fold strip in half along length to enclose raw edges. Edgestitch along both long sides to finish. Cut into two lengths of 16 cm. Stitch to robe front at side seam where comfortable, matching raw edges. Stitch centre back seam. Press.
3   Stitch shoulder seams, attaching stay-tape as you sew. Press. Stitch stay-tape to back neck edge to prevent stretching.

4   Stitch hood and yoke piece to robe around front and back neck. Stitch sleeves to body around armholes, matching notches. Press.
5   Stitch front to back from sleeve hem to robe hem, matching underarm points, and enclosing belt loops and pocket sides as you go. Press.
6   Turn under 10 cm at sleeve hem. Press. Topstitch. Turn under 10 cm at hood and front edge. Press. Turn hem up to suit. Press. Trim to 4 cm. Mitre corners at centre front hem. Topstitch around entire edge of robe to finish.
7   To make belt, stitch short ends together. Press. Fold in half along length, with right sides facing. Stitch around raw edges, leaving gap in middle for turning. Trim seam and corners. Turn to right side. Slipstitch gap closed. Press. Edgestitch belt to finish.

PYJAMAS

SIZE: M/L Man

MATERIALS

- ☐ **1.80 m of 150 cm wide cotton knit fabric**
- ☐ **10 cm of 70 cm wide ribbing**
- ☐ **50 cm narrow stay-tape for shoulder seams**
- ☐ **90 cm of 2 cm wide elastic**

PATTERN

See Pattern 15 for Top (V-neck, short sleeve). See Pattern 16 for pants (pyjama length)
Front Top (cut 1), Back Top (cut 1), Sleeve (cut 2), Front Leg (cut 2), Back Leg (cut 2), Neck Ribbing (cut 1).
Cut out pattern pieces as directed. 1 cm seams and 2 cm hems allowed. Join all pieces together with right sides facing. Exposed raw edges can be neatened by overlocking, zigzagging, or simply left raw, as knit fabric will not fray.

TO MAKE

Top:
1   Stitch shoulder seams, attaching stay-tape as you sew. Press.
2   Fold neck ribbing in half along length. Lay ends one on top of the other, in a neat V and matching raw edges. Pin evenly around neck with centre front points and raw edges matching. Stitch, snipping pyjama centre front point almost to stitching so you can stitch around the V. Press seam away from ribbing.

3   Stitch sleeves to body around armholes, matching notches. Press. Stitch
front to back along underarm seams,
matching underarm points. Press.
4   Turn under 2 cm at sleeve hem. Press.
Topstitch and edgestitch to finish. Turn
curved hem up to suit. Press. Trim to 2 cm.
Topstitch and edgestitch to finish.
Pants:
5   Stitch side seams. Press. Stitch inside
leg seams. Press. Stitch around crotch
seam from front waist to back waist, matching inside leg seam points. Press.
6   To form casing for elastic, turn under 3
cm at waist . Press. Stitch around waist 2.5
cm from edge, leaving gap at centre back
for inserting elastic. Cut elastic to fit waist,
insert and join ends. Stitch gap closed.
7   Turn hem up to suit. Press. Trim to 2
cm. Topstitch and edgestitch to finish.

HOODED ROBE

SIZE: M Man

MATERIALS
- ☐ **3.80 m of 150 cm wide stretch towelling fabric**
- ☐ **70 cm narrow stay-tape for shoulder seams and back neck**

PATTERN and TO MAKE
As for HOODED ROBE on page 47.

SLEEPSUIT

SIZE: 6 months

MATERIALS
- ☐ **80 cm of 150 cm wide stretch towelling fabric**
- ☐ **40 cm of 90 cm contrast stripe fabric for piping**
- ☐ **45 cm nylon zipper**
- ☐ **20 cm narrow elastic**

PATTERN and TO MAKE
As for SLEEPSUIT on page 23. Note that
we have used contrast bias piping instead
of self fabric. Be sure to cut the sleepsuit
pattern observing a one-way direction.

TRACKSUIT

SIZE: Age 6 months

MATERIALS, PATTERN and TO MAKE
As for TRACKSUIT on page 22.

TRACKSUIT

SIZE: Age 2 years

MATERIALS
- ☐ **1 m of 130 cm wide fleecy knit fabric**
- ☐ **30 cm of 88 cm wide ribbing**
- ☐ **60 cm of 2 cm wide elastic**

PATTERN
See Pattern 27
Cut ribbing as follows:
Neck, 6 cm long x 30 cm wide. Hipband,
10 cm long x 56 cm wide. Cuffs, two 10 cm
long x 13 cm wide. Ankles, two 10 cm long
x 16 cm wide. Piping, cut two 3 cm strips
across width of ribbing, to give you four 22
cm strips for armholes and two 44 cm
strips for legs.
Front Body (cut 1), Back Body (cut 1),
Sleeve (cut 2), Front Leg (cut 2), Back Leg
(cut 2).
Cut out pattern pieces as directed. 1 cm
seams allowed. Join all pieces together
with right sides facing. Exposed raw edges
can be neatened by overlocking, zigzagging, or simply left raw, as knit fabric will
not fray.

TO MAKE
As for TRACKSUIT on page 22.
(See picture, page 80)

PYJAMAS

SIZE: Age 6 years

MATERIALS
- ☐ **1 m of 150 cm wide cotton knit fabric**
- ☐ **30 cm of 90 cm wide ribbing**
- ☐ **30 cm narrow stay-tape for shoulder seams**
- ☐ **60 cm of 2 cm wide elastic**

PATTERN
See Pattern 9 for Top (low V-neck, curved
hem). See Pattern 10 for Pants (curved
hems)
Front Top (cut 1), Back Top (cut 1), Sleeve
(cut 2), Front Leg (cut 2), Back Leg (cut 2),
Neck Ribbing (cut 1). Cut ribbing in four 4
cm strips across width to give you two 20
cm strips for sleeve binding, two 54 cm
strips for leg bindings, and two 50 cm
strips for hem binding.
Cut out pattern pieces as directed. 1 cm
seams allowed. Join all pieces together
with right sides facing. Exposed raw edges
can be neatened by overlocking, zigzagging, or simply left raw, as knit fabric will
not fray.

TO MAKE
Top:
1   Stitch shoulder seams, attaching stay-
tape as you sew. Press.
2   Fold neck ribbing in half along length.
Lay ends one on top of the other, in a neat
V and matching raw edges. Pin evenly
around neck with centre front points and
raw edges matching. Stitch, snipping pyjama centre front point almost to stitching
so you can stitch around the V. Press
seam away from ribbing.
3   Stitch sleeves to body around armholes, matching notches. Press. Stitch

front to back along underarm seams, matching underarm points. Press.

4   Stitch short ends of sleeve binding. Press seam, fold in half along length. With join at underarm, pin binding evenly around lower edge of sleeve with raw edges even and right sides facing. Stitch. Press seam away from binding. Edgestitch to finish. Make curved hem bindings in the same manner, placing joins at side seams.

Pants:

5   Stitch side seams. Press. Stitch inside leg seams. Press. Stitch around crotch seam from front waist to back waist, matching inside leg seam points. Press.

6   To form casing for elastic, turn under 3 cm at waist edge. Press. Stitch around waist 2.5 cm from edge, leaving gap at centre back for inserting elastic. Cut elastic to fit waist, insert and join ends. Stitch gap closed.

7   Make curved hem bindings in the same manner as top, placing joins at side seams.

NIGHTIE

SIZE: Age 6 years

MATERIALS
- ☐ **90 cm of 150 cm wide cotton knit fabric**
- ☐ **20 cm of 90 cm wide ribbing**
- ☐ **30 cm narrow stay-tape for shoulder seams**

PATTERN

See Pattern 9 (low V-neck, long length) Front (cut 1), Back (cut 1), Sleeve (cut 2), Neck Ribbing (cut 1). Cut ribbing in two 4 cm strips across width to give you two 20 cm strips for sleeve binding, and two 50 cm strips for hem binding.

Cut out pattern pieces as directed. 1 cm seams allowed. Join all pieces together with right sides facing. Exposed raw edges can be neatened by overlocking, zigzag-

ging, or simply left raw, as knit fabric will not fray.

TO MAKE

As for PYJAMAS (top only) on page 48.

Patterns

HOW TO SECTION

Well – have we inspired you? It really is as easy as it looks, and this information will make using our patterns a simple task.

There are always choices to be made before any pattern is used and these pointers will help.

TO ALTER THE PATTERN, OR TO MAKE DO?

Almost no-one is a standard size, so altering a pattern, even if it is only the hem length, is a common decision. Length and width are the most usual alterations, so let's cover them both.

Length: Hems can be lengthened or shortened. Sleeves and legs should be lengthened or shortened at about elbow and knee positions. Simply split the pattern piece, spread the upper and lower pieces apart, or overlap them, as necessary. Then cut out the fabric. If you do lengthen a garment, note on the pattern pieces the amount you have added – it's easy to forget!

To decrease the length in body pieces follow the same principles as for legs and arms. This is often achievable by simply creasing out excess length in a pattern piece and holding it against yourself for testing. Lengthening body pieces should be done where no joining piece will be interfered with – that is, do not lengthen across the chest at the sleeve line unless you add more length to the top of your sleeve or the sleeve will not fit! It's best to lower the alteration line to below the bust or chest where a clear line is achievable.

Width: Altering width in a pattern piece can be a slightly more involved process than lengthening. But don't be put off! Side seams are simply widened by adding the required amount to the pattern side seams before cutting out. Be sure to observe the line of the side and not alter the basic shape, that is, add a uniform amount the full length of the seam. To alter width across the shoulders, split the centre of the shoulder down to the bustline and spread the pattern out by the required amount. This will alter your armhole slightly, and you will have to re-curve the shape of the armhole. You can also split the entire garment down from the shoulder, then spread it the required amount. These processes may sound difficult, but as soon as you try them for yourself all will become clear.

Sizing is a well-known danger area in sewing. How often have you sewn something, in your usual size, and found that it was either best suited to fit three of you, or only half of you? Always measure the pattern first with your own measurements in mind, then remembering the above ideas about alteration, alter to suit yourself.

Never assume that the size stated is the size just right for you! Treat it as a guide, but let your tapemeasure be your friend.

HOW TO CREATE PAPER PATTERNS

At the back of the book is a tear-out grid sheet. Lay this flat on a table, smoothing the creases out. Place joined widths of kitchen wrap, or dressmaker's tissue paper over the grid and proceed to copy from the gridded patterns in the book. The aim is to transfer the pattern as it is shown in the book to the tissue paper you are drawing on. Because the grid underneath the pattern is of the correct size – 2.5 cm square – the pattern will, when copied, be of the correct dimensions. Copy the pattern lines square by square. Try placing a dot at every spot where the pattern lines cross a grid line, then connecting the dots. Childsplay!

Another angle to consider is photocopying. Copy the patterns and enlarge continuously until the correct dimensions are achieved. This method could save you time and effort if photocopying facilities are available to you. If you will be using patterns again and again cut them from non-adhesive interfacing. This does not tear or become tatty as paper does, and pattern labels can be written with ease.

FABRIC CHOICES

Colour is probably the first element that will attract you when choosing fabric, and this is correct. However, one of the more important elements to consider is the weight of the fabric. Stretch fabrics come in a wide variety of weights: heavy, fluffy fabrics just right for winter tracksuits, lightweight cotton knits perfect for baby's sleepsuit – the list goes on.

You must make two decisions when choosing fabrics - is the weight suitable for what you wish to make, and is your machine capable of handling this weight? Machines can generally handle most fabrics, but be aware of possible problems. Will you be able to handle the bulk of this fabric, or can you control this very slippery fabric? This advice is not intended to alarm you, but should alert you to the problems of choosing a fabric difficult to handle.

As you progress with stretch fabric sewing, your ability to cope with these problems will increase. Remember, progress slowly and don't take too many shortcuts – and very soon you'll be an expert.

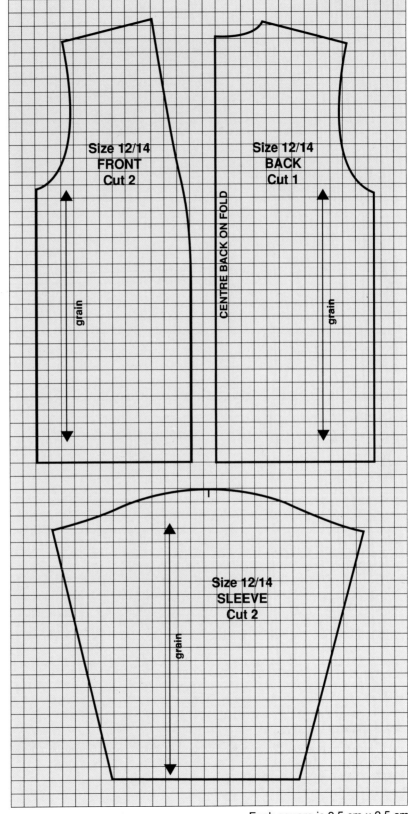

Size 12/14
FRONT
Cut 2

grain

Size 12/14
BACK
Cut 1

CENTRE BACK ON FOLD

grain

Size 12/14
SLEEVE
Cut 2

grain

Each square is 2.5 cm x 2.5 cm

Pattern 2 is on page 71

DOLMAN SLEEVED TUNIC / DOLMAN SLEEVED DRESS (BACK)

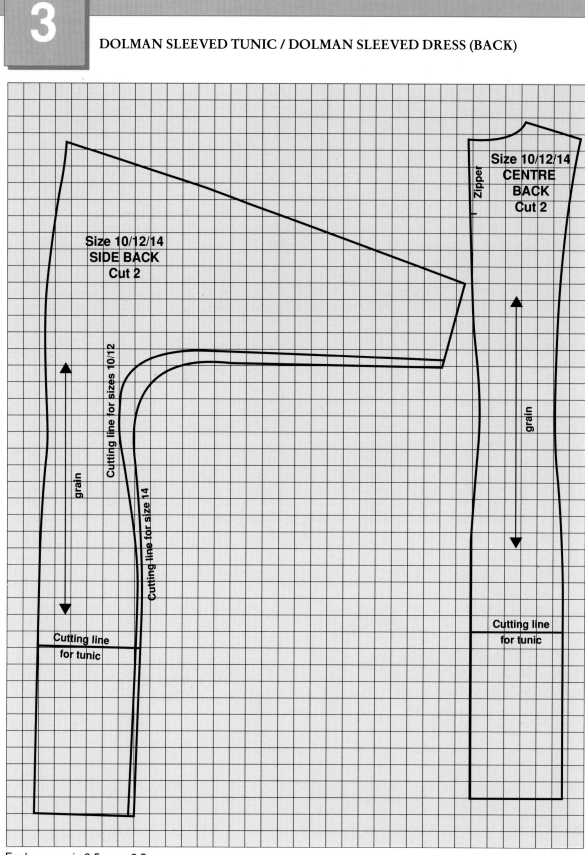

Size 10/12/14
SIDE BACK
Cut 2

Size 10/12/14
CENTRE BACK
Cut 2

Zipper

grain

grain

Cutting line for sizes 10/12

Cutting line for size 14

Cutting line for tunic

Cutting line for tunic

Each square is 2.5 cm x 2.5 cm

DOLMAN SLEEVED TUNIC / DOLMAN SLEEVED DRESS (FRONT)

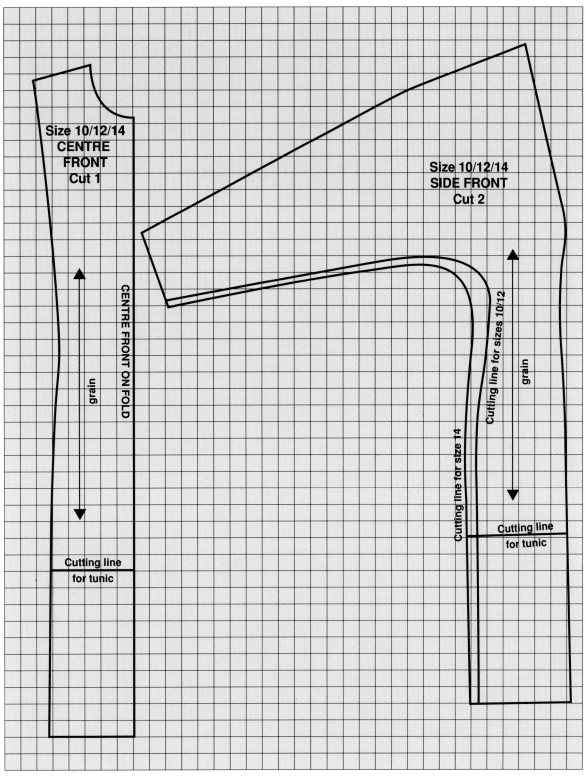

Size 10/12/14
CENTRE FRONT
Cut 1

grain

CENTRE FRONT ON FOLD

Cutting line for tunic

Size 10/12/14
SIDE FRONT
Cut 2

grain

Cutting line for sizes 10/12

Cutting line for size 14

Cutting line for tunic

Each square is 2.5 cm x 2.5 cm

CENTRE FRONT

CENTRE BACK

grain

Size 10/12
FRONT AND BACK LEG
Cut 2

Each square is 2.5 cm x 2.5 cm

SWEATSHIRT / T-SHIRT NIGHTIE

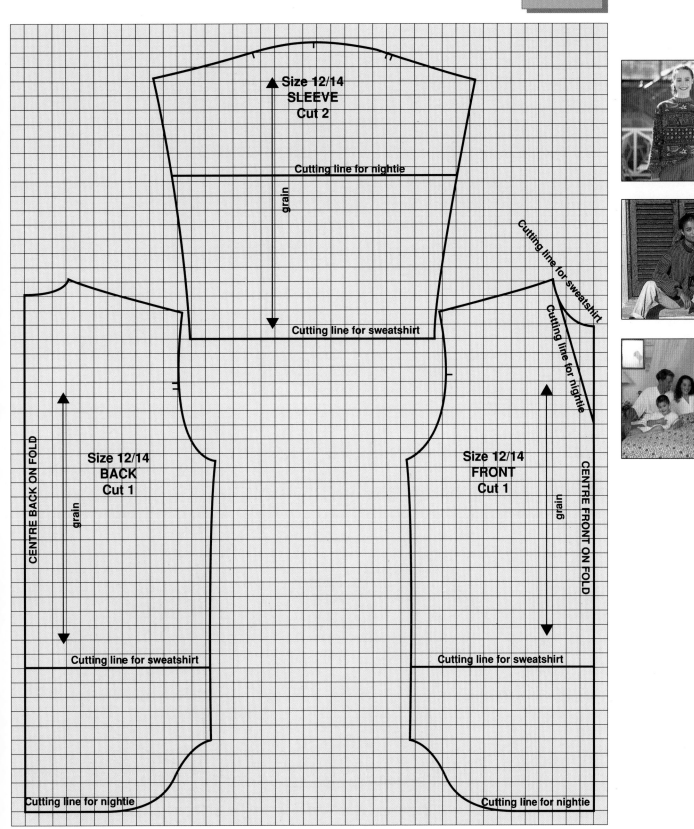

Size 12/14
SLEEVE
Cut 2

grain

Cutting line for nightie

Cutting line for sweatshirt

Cutting line for sweatshirt

Cutting line for nightie

CENTRE BACK ON FOLD

grain

Size 12/14
BACK
Cut 1

Size 12/14
FRONT
Cut 1

grain

CENTRE FRONT ON FOLD

Cutting line for sweatshirt

Cutting line for sweatshirt

Cutting line for nightie

Cutting line for nightie

Each square is 2.5 cm x 2.5 cm

EIGHT GORE SKIRT

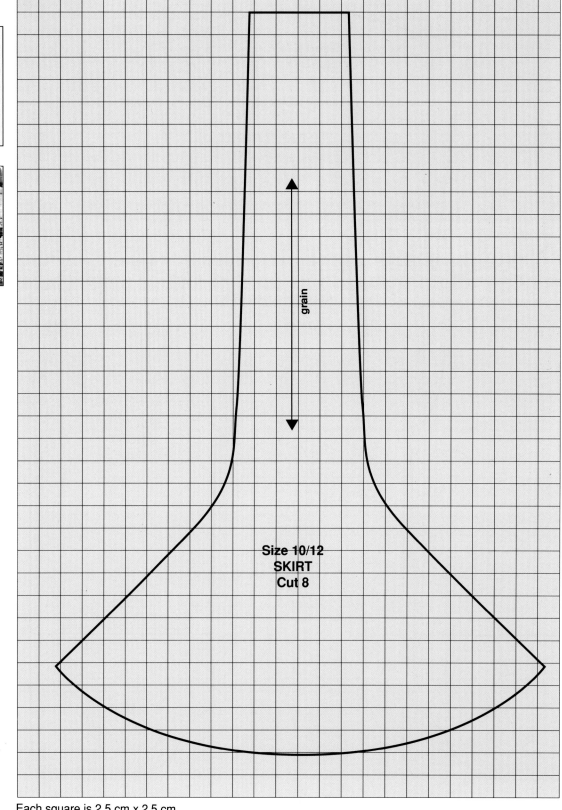

grain

**Size 10/12
SKIRT
Cut 8**

Each square is 2.5 cm x 2.5 cm

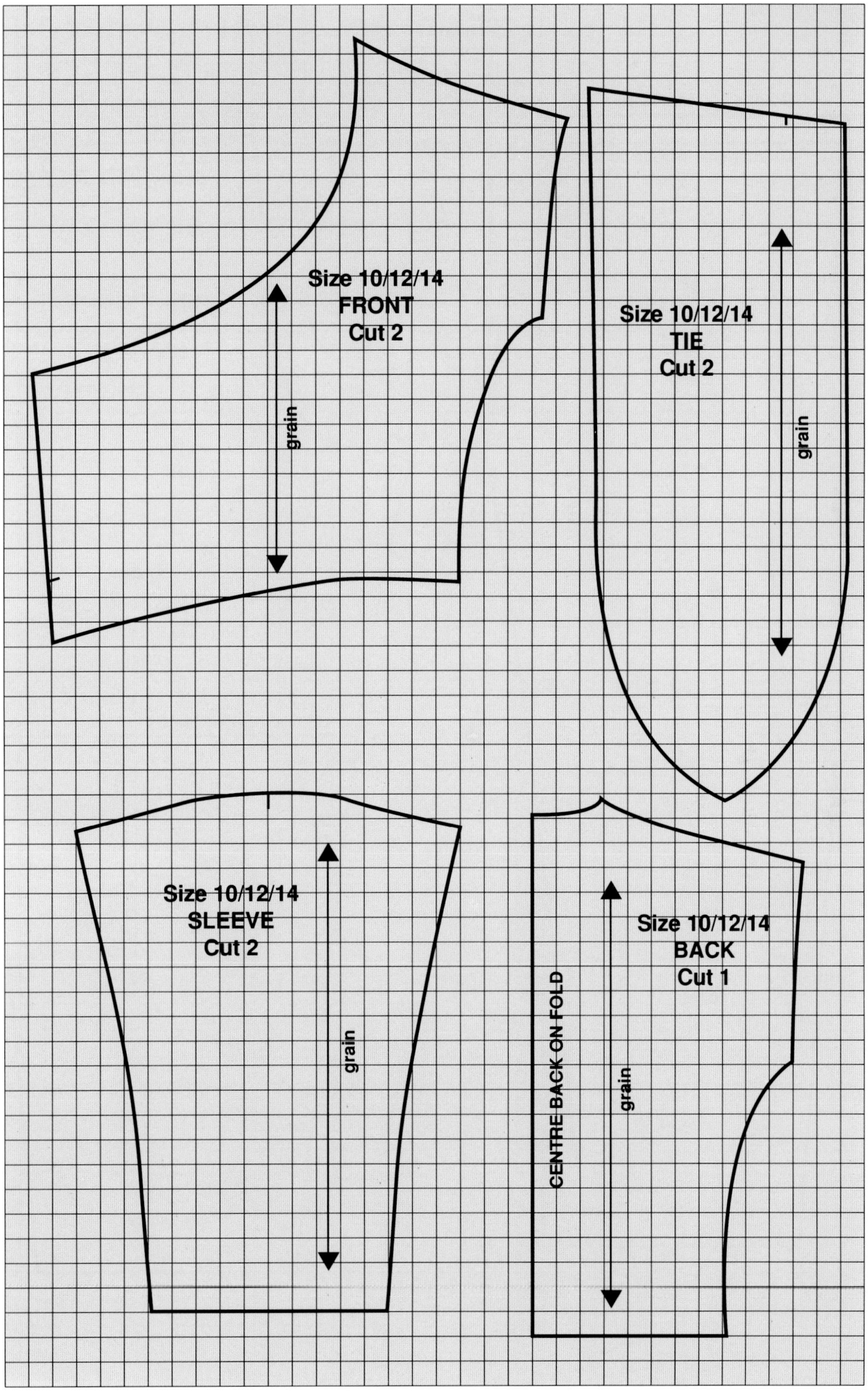

Size 10/12/14
FRONT
Cut 2

grain

Size 10/12/14
TIE
Cut 2

grain

Size 10/12/14
SLEEVE
Cut 2

grain

Size 10/12/14
BACK
Cut 1

CENTRE BACK ON FOLD

grain

Each square is 2.5 cm x 2.5 cm

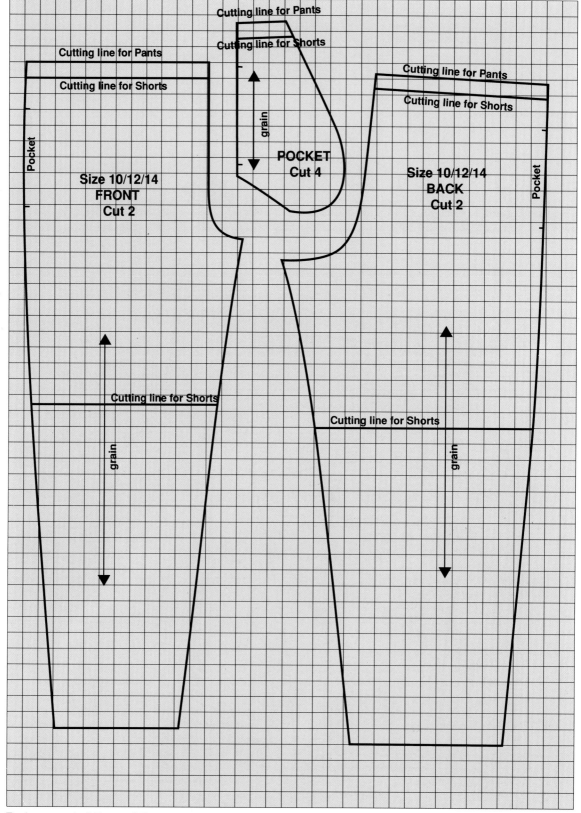

Cutting line for Pants

Cutting line for Shorts

Cutting line for Pants

Cutting line for Shorts

Pocket

grain

POCKET
Cut 4

Size 10/12/14
FRONT
Cut 2

Cutting line for Pants

Cutting line for Shorts

Size 10/12/14
BACK
Cut 2

Pocket

grain

Cutting line for Shorts

Cutting line for Shorts

grain

grain

Each square is 2.5 cm x 2.5 cm

V T-SHIRT / T-SHIRT WITH RIBBING / T-SHIRT / PYJAMA TOP / NIGHTIE

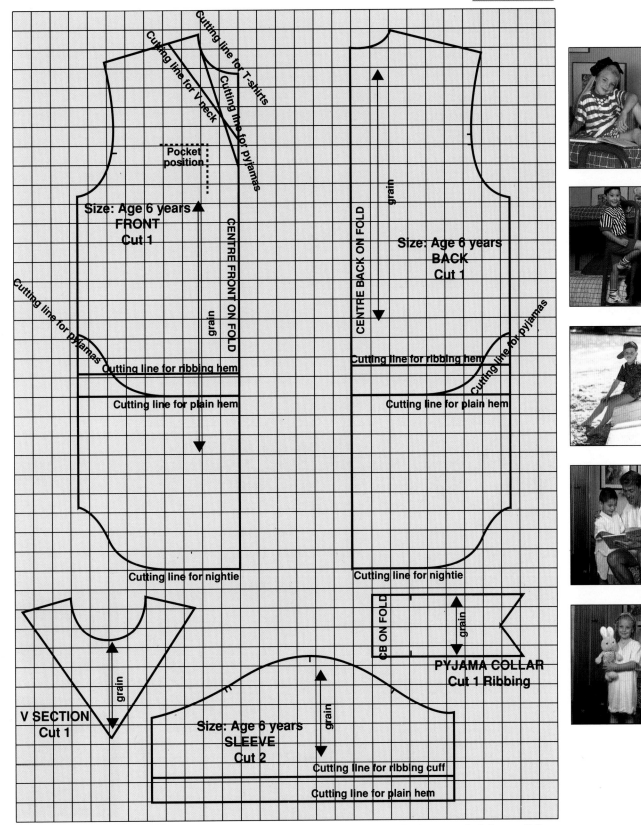

Cutting line for T-shirts

Cutting line for V-neck

Cutting line for pyjamas

Pocket position

Size: Age 6 years
FRONT
Cut 1

CENTRE FRONT ON FOLD

grain

Cutting line for pyjamas

Cutting line for ribbing hem

Cutting line for plain hem

Cutting line for nightie

grain

CENTRE BACK ON FOLD

Size: Age 6 years
BACK
Cut 1

Cutting line for ribbing hem

Cutting line for pyjamas

Cutting line for plain hem

Cutting line for nightie

V SECTION
Cut 1

grain

Size: Age 6 years
SLEEVE
Cut 2

grain

CB ON FOLD

grain

PYJAMA COLLAR
Cut 1 Ribbing

Cutting line for ribbing cuff

Cutting line for plain hem

Each square is 2.5 cm x 2.5 cm

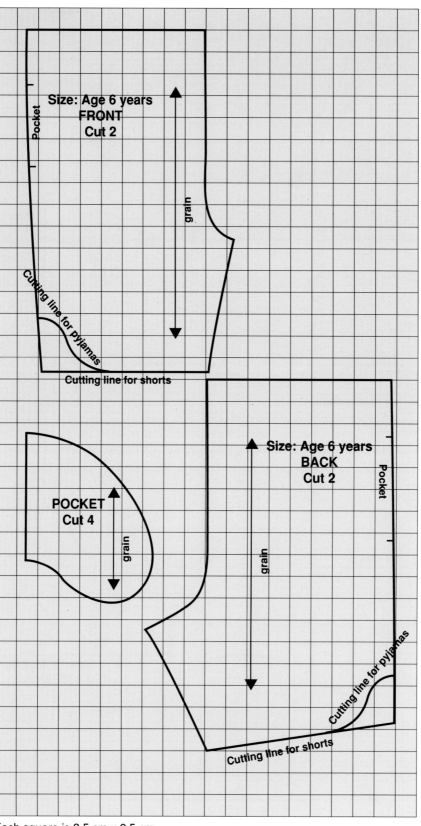

Pocket

Size: Age 6 years
FRONT
Cut 2

grain

Cutting line for pyjamas

Cutting line for shorts

POCKET
Cut 4

grain

Size: Age 6 years
BACK
Cut 2

Pocket

grain

Cutting line for pyjamas

Cutting line for shorts

Each square is 2.5 cm x 2.5 cm

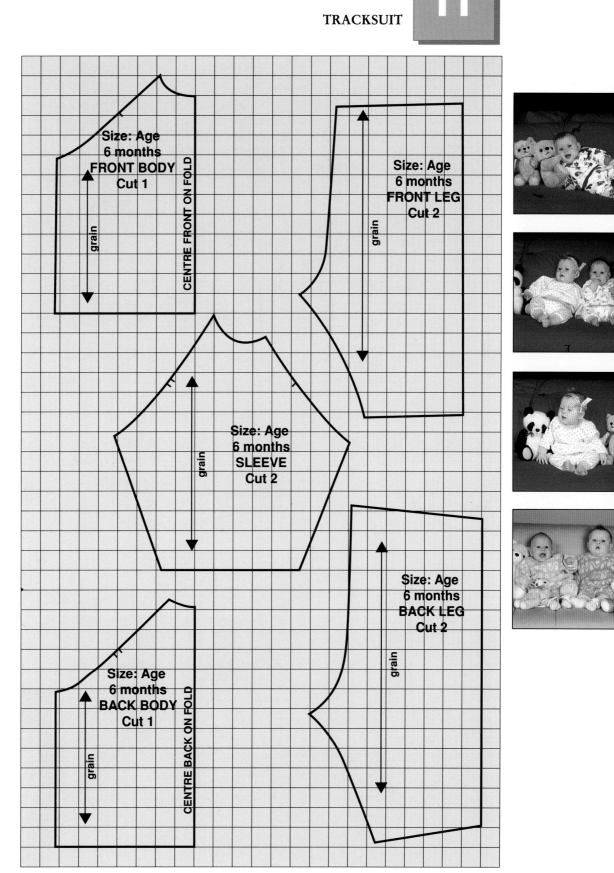

**Size: Age
6 months
FRONT BODY
Cut 1**

grain

CENTRE FRONT ON FOLD

**Size: Age
6 months
FRONT LEG
Cut 2**

grain

**Size: Age
6 months
SLEEVE
Cut 2**

grain

**Size: Age
6 months
BACK LEG
Cut 2**

grain

**Size: Age
6 months
BACK BODY
Cut 1**

grain

CENTRE BACK ON FOLD

Each square is 2.5 cm x 2.5 cm

VEST AND PANTS

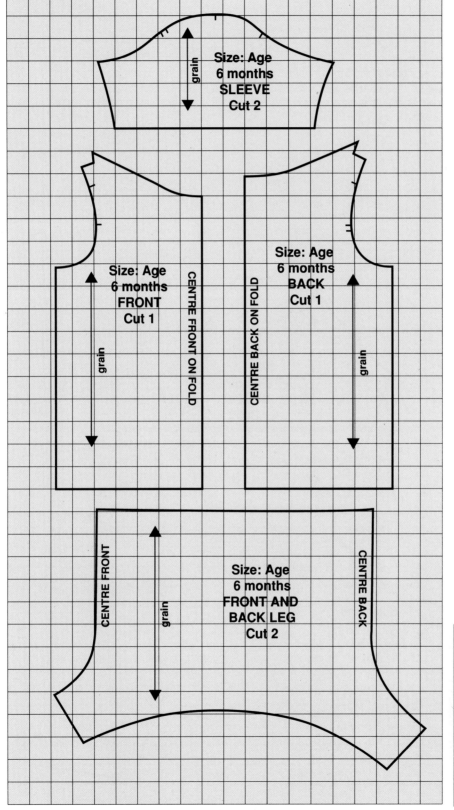

Size: Age
6 months
SLEEVE
Cut 2

grain

Size: Age
6 months
FRONT
Cut 1

CENTRE FRONT ON FOLD

CENTRE BACK ON FOLD

Size: Age
6 months
BACK
Cut 1

grain

CENTRE FRONT

CENTRE BACK

grain

Size: Age
6 months
FRONT AND
BACK LEG
Cut 2

Each square is 2.5 cm x 2.5 cm

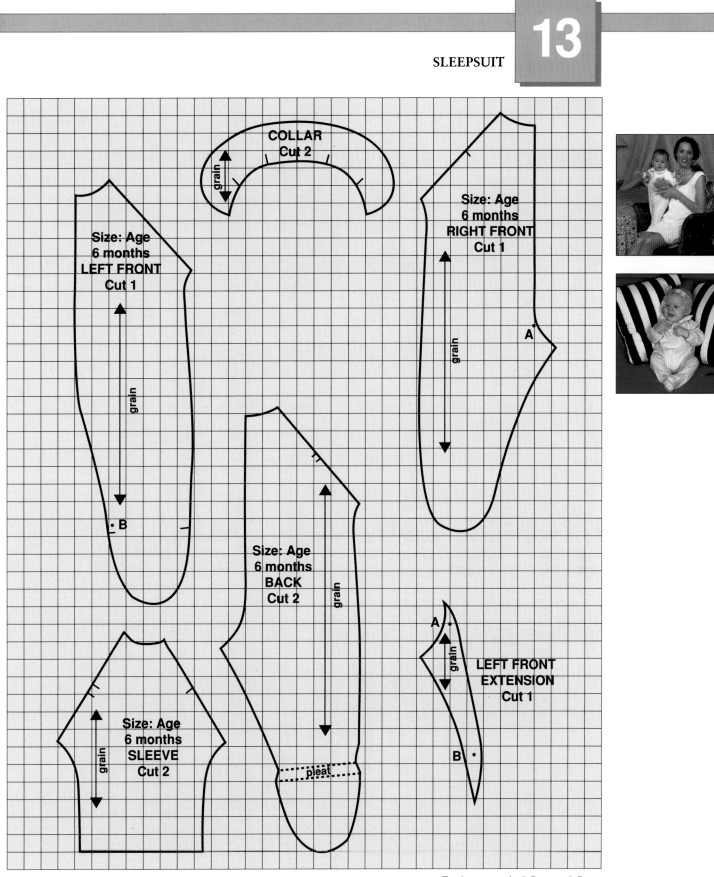

COLLAR
Cut 2

grain

Size: Age
6 months
LEFT FRONT
Cut 1

grain

• B

Size: Age
6 months
RIGHT FRONT
Cut 1

grain

A

Size: Age
6 months
BACK
Cut 2

grain

A •
grain

LEFT FRONT
EXTENSION
Cut 1

B •

Size: Age
6 months
SLEEVE
Cut 2

grain

pleat

Each square is 2.5 cm x 2.5 cm

COLOUR BLOCK TRACKSUIT

UPPER RIGHT BACK
Cut 1
UPPER LEFT BACK (reverse)
Cut 1

grain

Size: Age 4 years
SLEEVE
Cut 2

grain

UPPER LEFT FRONT
Cut 1
UPPER RIGHT FRONT (reverse)
Cut 1

grain

LOWER RIGHT BACK
Cut 1
LOWER LEFT BACK (reverse)
Cut 1

grain

CENTRE BACK

CENTRE FRONT

Size: Age 4 years
FRONT AND BACK LEG
Cut 2

grain

LOWER LEFT FRONT
Cut 1
LOWER RIGHT FRONT (reverse)
Cut 1

grain

Each square is 2.5 cm x 2.5 cm

T-SHIRT / SWEATSHIRT / PYJAMA TOP

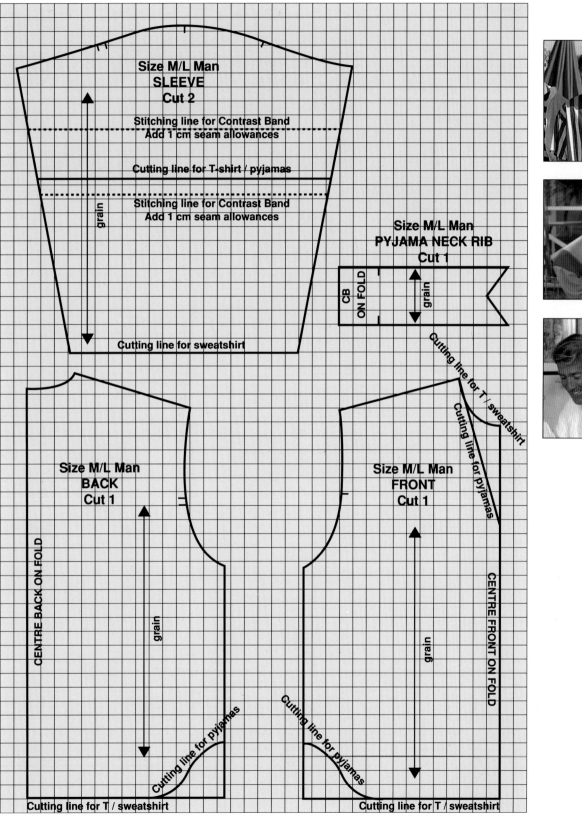

Size M/L Man
SLEEVE
Cut 2

Stitching line for Contrast Band
Add 1 cm seam allowances

Cutting line for T-shirt / pyjamas

Stitching line for Contrast Band
Add 1 cm seam allowances

grain

Cutting line for sweatshirt

Size M/L Man
PYJAMA NECK RIB
Cut 1

CB ON FOLD

grain

Cutting line for T / sweatshirt

Cutting line for pyjamas

Size M/L Man
BACK
Cut 1

CENTRE BACK ON FOLD

grain

Size M/L Man
FRONT
Cut 1

CENTRE FRONT ON FOLD

grain

Cutting line for pyjamas

Cutting line for pyjamas

Cutting line for T / sweatshirt

Cutting line for T / sweatshirt

Each square is 2.5 cm x 2.5 cm

SHORTS / SPORT SHORTS / TRACK PANTS / PYJAMA PANTS

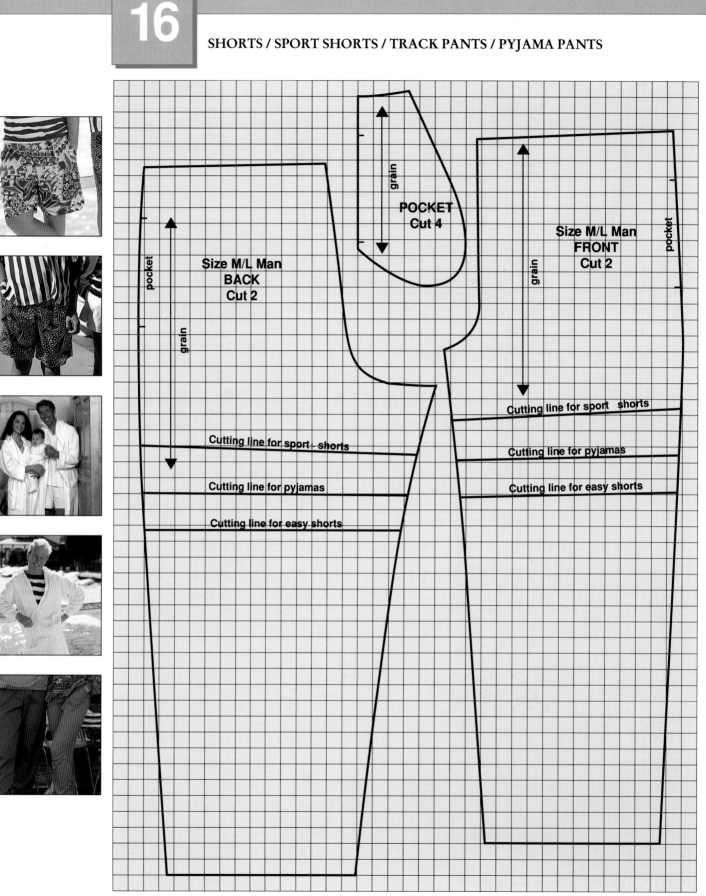

POCKET
Cut 4

grain

pocket

Size M/L Man
BACK
Cut 2

grain

Size M/L Man
FRONT
Cut 2

grain

pocket

Cutting line for sport   shorts

Cutting line for sport shorts

Cutting line for pyjamas

Cutting line for pyjamas

Cutting line for easy shorts

Cutting line for easy shorts

Each square is 2.5 cm x 2.5 cm

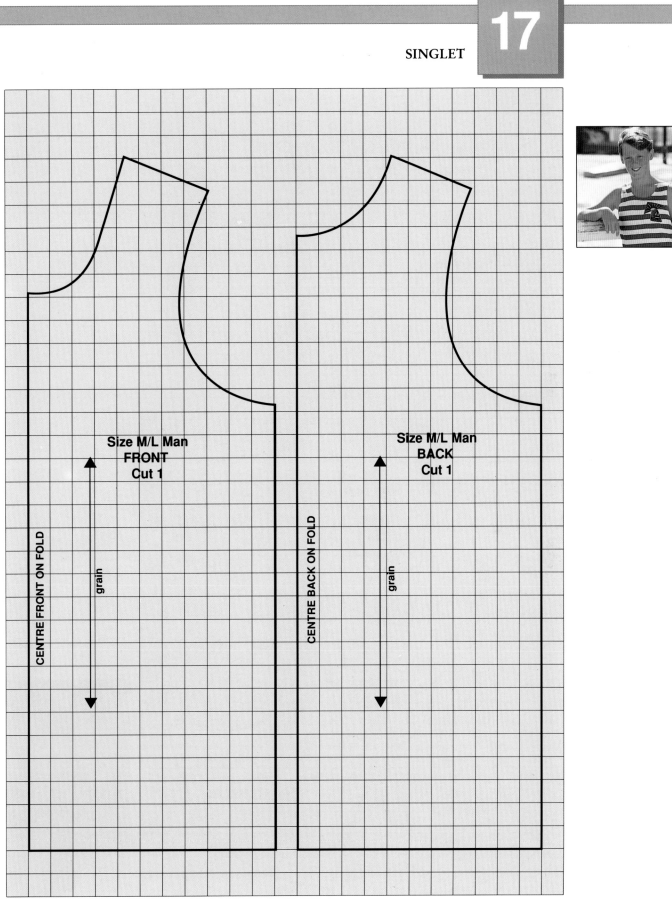

Size M/L Man
FRONT
Cut 1

CENTRE FRONT ON FOLD

grain

Size M/L Man
BACK
Cut 1

CENTRE BACK ON FOLD

grain

Each square is 2.5 cm x 2.5 cm

PANELLED SWIMSUIT

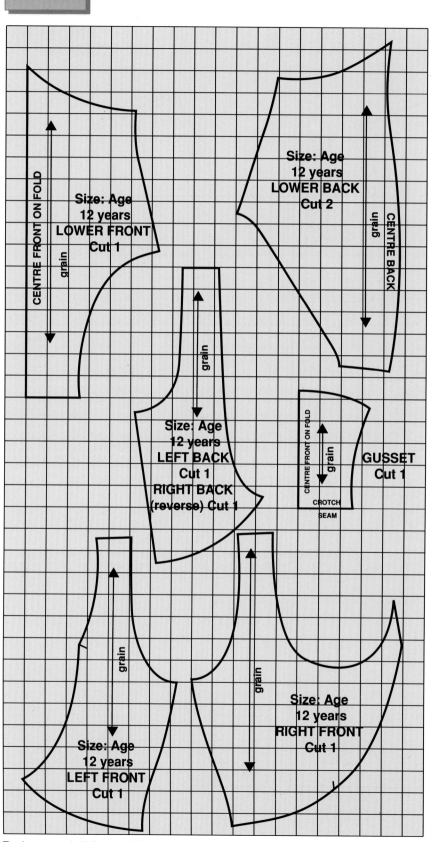

Size: Age
12 years
LOWER FRONT
Cut 1

CENTRE FRONT ON FOLD

grain

Size: Age
12 years
LOWER BACK
Cut 2

grain

CENTRE BACK

grain

Size: Age
12 years
LEFT BACK
Cut 1
RIGHT BACK
(reverse) Cut 1

CENTRE FRONT ON FOLD

grain

GUSSET
Cut 1

CROTCH
SEAM

grain

Size: Age
12 years
LEFT FRONT
Cut 1

grain

Size: Age
12 years
RIGHT FRONT
Cut 1

Each square is 2.5 cm x 2.5 cm

MAN'S RAGLAN JACKET / MAN'S AND LADY'S SQUARE NECK TOP

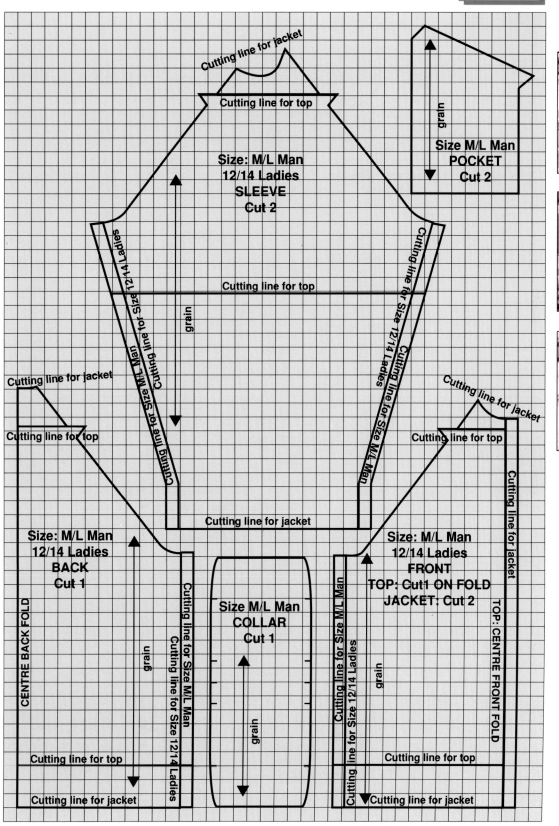

Cutting line for jacket

Cutting line for top

**Size: M/L Man
12/14 Ladies
SLEEVE
Cut 2**

Cutting line for Size 12/14 Ladies

Cutting line for Size M/L Man

Cutting line for top

grain

Cutting line for Size 12/14 Ladies

Cutting line for Size M/L Man

**Size M/L Man
POCKET
Cut 2**

grain

Cutting line for jacket

Cutting line for top

Cutting line for jacket

Cutting line for top

Cutting line for jacket

Cutting line for jacket

**Size: M/L Man
12/14 Ladies
BACK
Cut 1**

CENTRE BACK FOLD

grain

Cutting line for Size M/L Man

Cutting line for Size 12/14 Ladies

**Size M/L Man
COLLAR
Cut 1**

grain

Cutting line for Size M/L Man

Cutting line for Size 12/14 Ladies

grain

**Size: M/L Man
12/14 Ladies
FRONT
TOP: Cut1 ON FOLD
JACKET: Cut 2**

TOP: CENTRE FRONT FOLD

Cutting line for top

Cutting line for jacket

Cutting line for top

Cutting line for jacket

Each square is 2.5 cm x 2.5 cm

SINGLET TOP / SINGLET DRESS

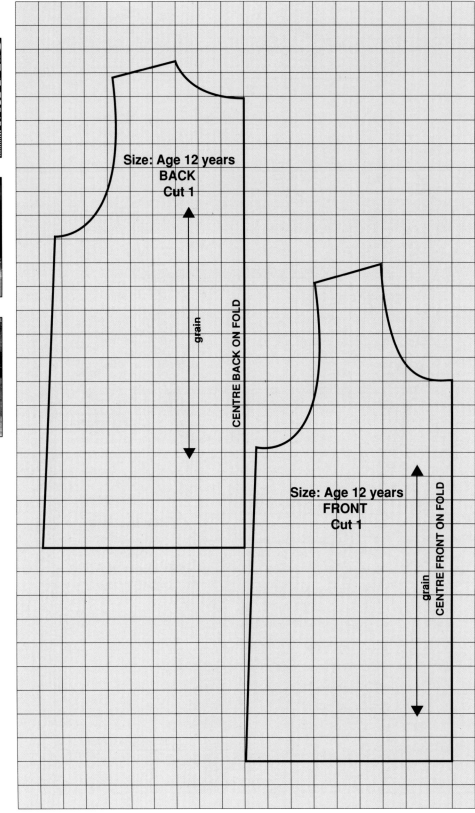

Size: Age 12 years
BACK
Cut 1

grain

CENTRE BACK ON FOLD

Size: Age 12 years
FRONT
Cut 1

grain
CENTRE FRONT ON FOLD

Each square is 2.5 cm x 2.5 cm

SWIM TRUNKS

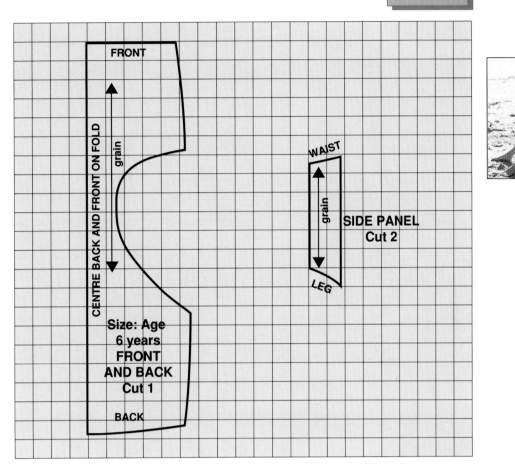

FRONT

CENTRE BACK AND FRONT ON FOLD

grain

WAIST

grain

SIDE PANEL
Cut 2

LEG

Size: Age
6 years
FRONT
AND BACK
Cut 1

BACK

2

POCKET BAG

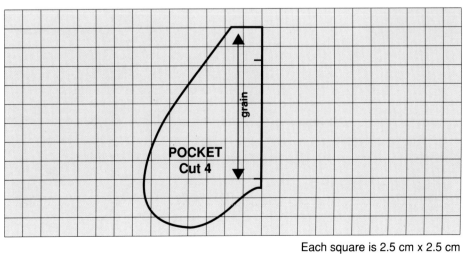

grain

POCKET
Cut 4

Each square is 2.5 cm x 2.5 cm

STITCHED SWIMSUIT

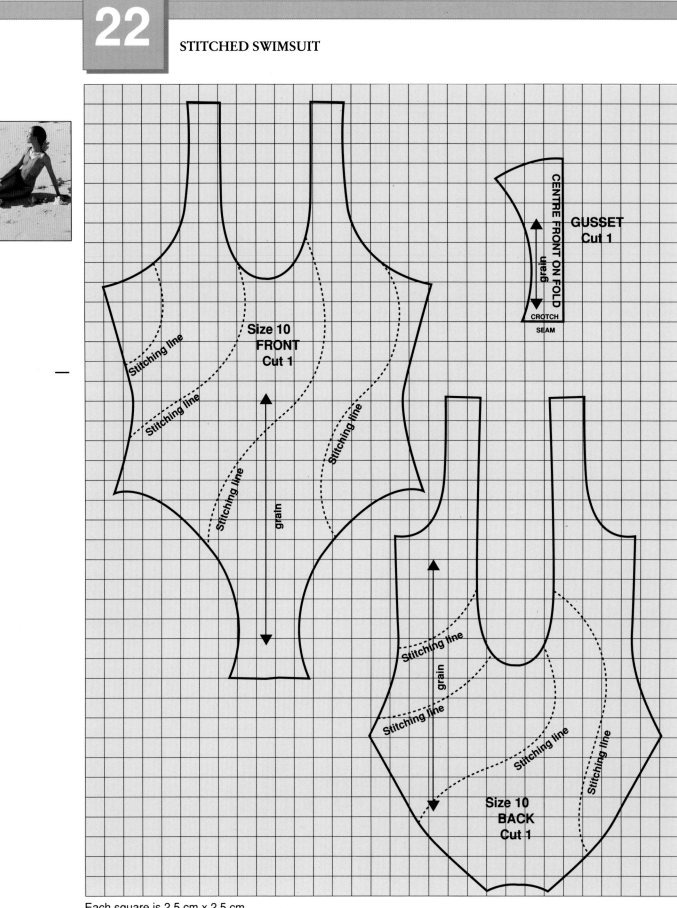

GUSSET
Cut 1

CENTRE FRONT ON FOLD

grain

CROTCH

SEAM

Stitching line

Size 10
FRONT
Cut 1

Stitching line

Stitching line

Stitching line

grain

Stitching line

grain

Stitching line

Stitching line

Stitching line

Size 10
BACK
Cut 1

Each square is 2.5 cm x 2.5 cm

23

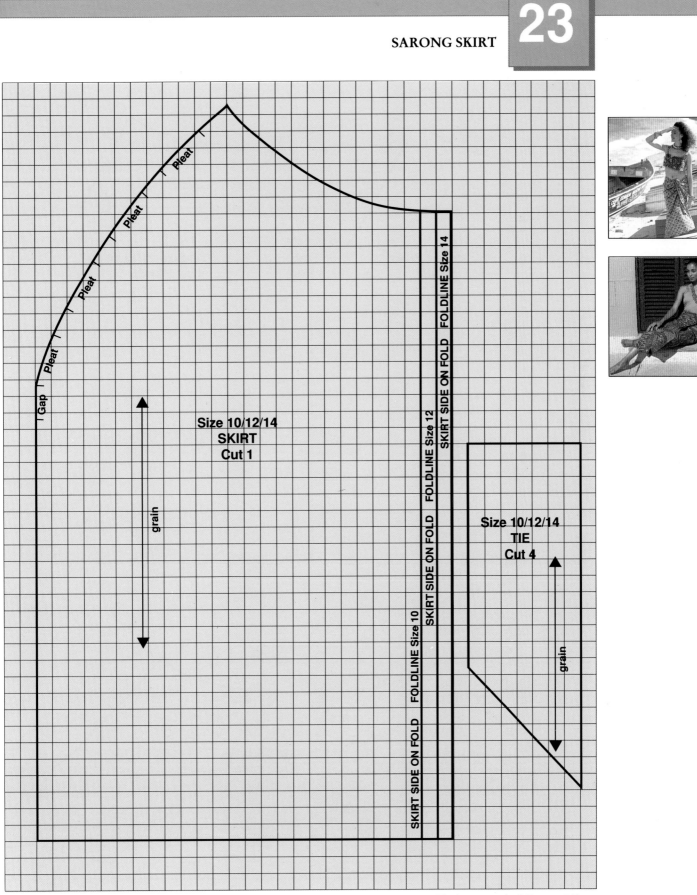

Pleat
Pleat
Pleat
Pleat
Pleat
Gap | Pleat

Size 10/12/14
SKIRT
Cut 1

grain

SKIRT SIDE ON FOLD — FOLDLINE Size 10

SKIRT SIDE ON FOLD — FOLDLINE Size 12

SKIRT SIDE ON FOLD — FOLDLINE Size 14

Size 10/12/14
TIE
Cut 4

grain

Each square is 2.5 cm x 2.5 cm

GYPSY TOP

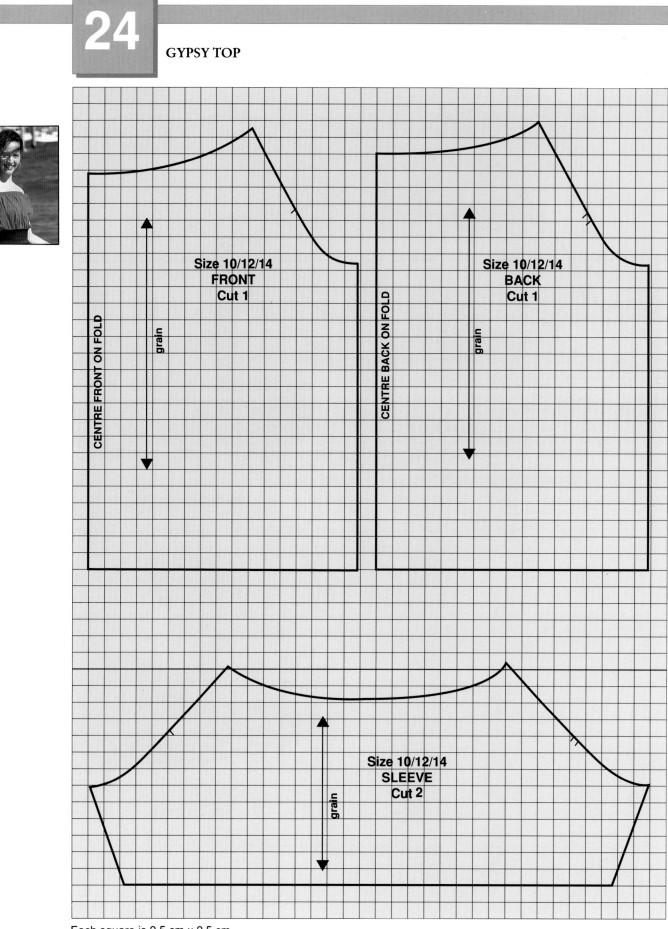

Size 10/12/14
FRONT
Cut 1

CENTRE FRONT ON FOLD

grain

Size 10/12/14
BACK
Cut 1

CENTRE BACK ON FOLD

grain

Size 10/12/14
SLEEVE
Cut 2

grain

Each square is 2.5 cm x 2.5 cm

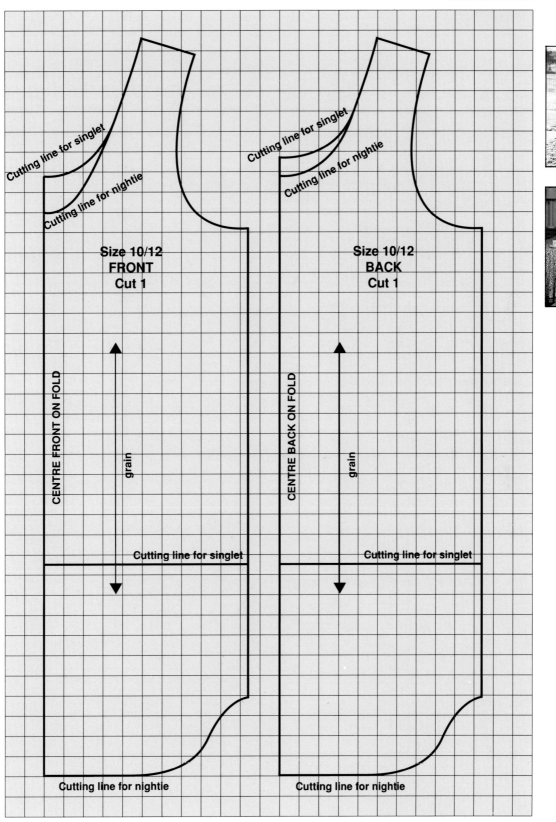

Cutting line for singlet

Cutting line for nightie

Cutting line for singlet

Cutting line for nightie

**Size 10/12
FRONT
Cut 1**

**Size 10/12
BACK
Cut 1**

CENTRE FRONT ON FOLD

CENTRE BACK ON FOLD

grain

grain

Cutting line for singlet

Cutting line for singlet

Cutting line for nightie

Cutting line for nightie

Each square is 2.5 cm x 2.5 cm

SHORT SINGLET TOP

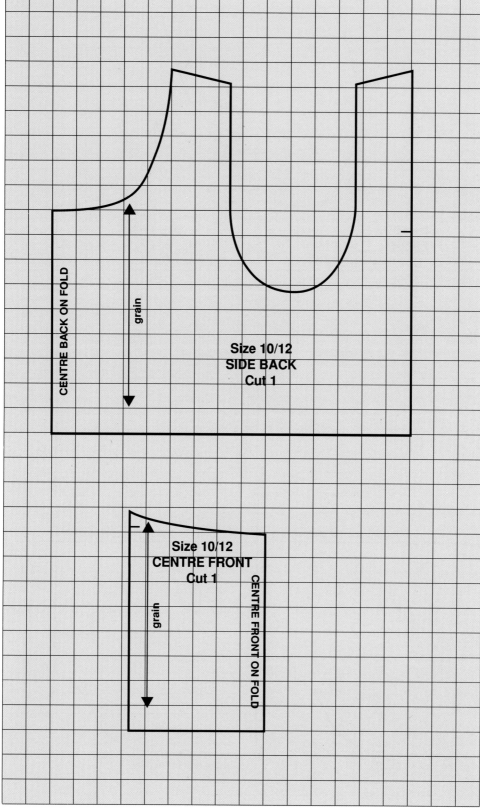

CENTRE BACK ON FOLD

grain

Size 10/12
SIDE BACK
Cut 1

Size 10/12
CENTRE FRONT
Cut 1

grain

CENTRE FRONT ON FOLD

Each square is 2.5 cm x 2.5 cm

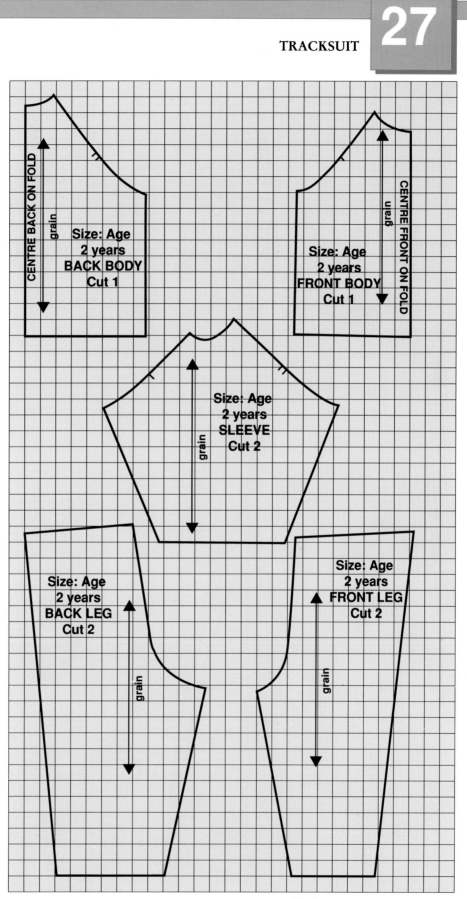

CENTRE BACK ON FOLD

grain

**Size: Age
2 years
BACK BODY
Cut 1**

CENTRE FRONT ON FOLD

grain

**Size: Age
2 years
FRONT BODY
Cut 1**

grain

**Size: Age
2 years
SLEEVE
Cut 2**

**Size: Age
2 years
BACK LEG
Cut 2**

grain

**Size: Age
2 years
FRONT LEG
Cut 2**

grain

Each square is 2.5 cm x 2.5 cm

MAN'S HOODED ROBE, LADY'S HOODED ROBE (BACK)

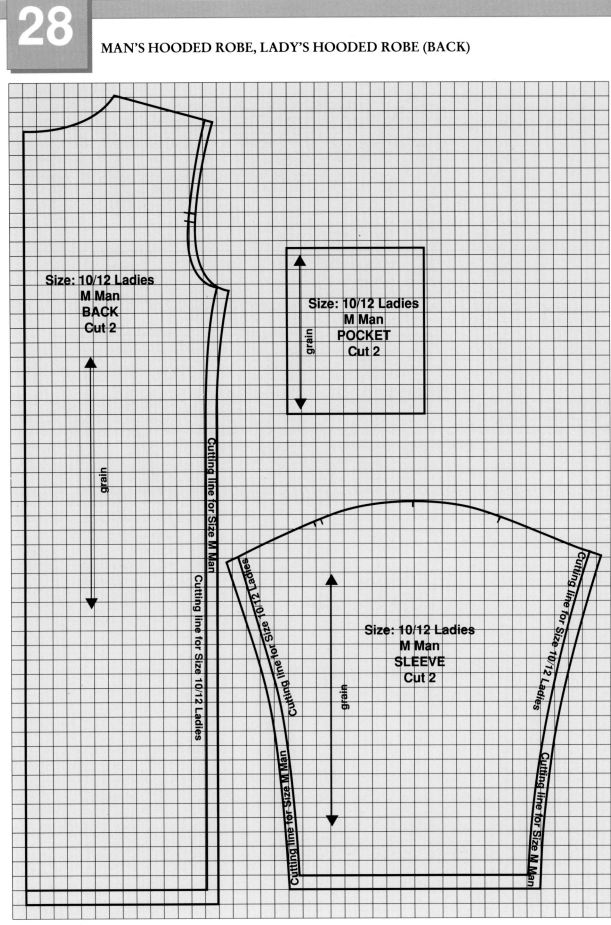

Size: 10/12 Ladies
M Man
BACK
Cut 2

grain

Cutting line for Size M Man

Cutting line for Size 10/12 Ladies

Size: 10/12 Ladies
M Man
POCKET
Cut 2

grain

Size: 10/12 Ladies
M Man
SLEEVE
Cut 2

grain

Cutting line for Size 10/12 Ladies

Cutting line for Size M Man

Cutting line for Size M Man

Cutting line for Size 10/12 Ladies

Each square is 2.5 cm x 2.5 cm

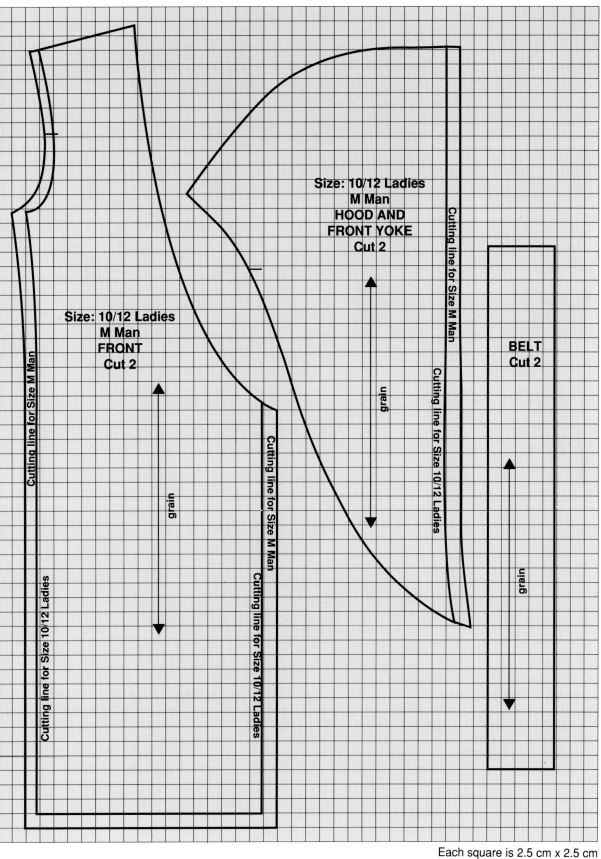

Size: 10/12 Ladies
M Man
HOOD AND
FRONT YOKE
Cut 2

grain

Cutting line for Size M Man

Cutting line for Size 10/12 Ladies

Size: 10/12 Ladies
M Man
FRONT
Cut 2

grain

Cutting line for Size M Man

Cutting line for Size 10/12 Ladies

Cutting line for Size M Man

Cutting line for Size 10/12 Ladies

BELT
Cut 2

grain

Each square is 2.5 cm x 2.5 cm

Warm tracksuit or snuggly pyjamas for a two-year old. See page 48

ACKNOWLEDGEMENTS

For their generous supply of fabric for these garments, we wish to thank Just Knits, Sydney, Australia (02) 669 6400 (pages 18 to 35 and page 48), and Hill Textiles, Sydney, Australia (02) 648 5888 (pages 8 to 17 and 36 to 49)

Fabric was also supplied by Home Yardage, Sydney

Garments were sewn on Bernina and Pfaff sewing machines

For photographic locations, our thanks to:
Dunbar House/Fisherman's Lodge, Watsons Bay, Sydney, Australia (02) 337 1226
Freedom Furniture, Surry Hills, Sydney, Australia (02) 331 3070
Doyles Restaurant, Watsons Bay, Sydney, Australia (02) 337 2007

Toys from The Fantastic Toy Shop, Sydney, Australia (02) 232 2318
Hats from Christies Uniforms, Sydney, Australia (02) 264 6751
Jewellery by African Heritage, Darlinghurst, Sydney, Australia (02) 283 1939, and Merivale, Sydney, Australia (02) 264 7000
Shoes by Reebok, socks by Red Robin